STUDIES IN ENGLISH LITERATURES

Edited by Koray Melikoğlu

Maria Festa

History and Race in Caryl Phillips's *The Nature of Blood*

STUDIES IN ENGLISH LITERATURES
Edited by Koray Melikoğlu
ISSN 1614-4651

11   *Annie Gagiano*
Dealing with Evils
Essays on Writing from Africa
2nd, revised and expanded edition
ISBN 978-3-89821-867-2

12   *Thomas F. Halloran*
James Joyce: Developing Irish Identity
A Study of the Development of Postcolonial Irish Identity in the Novels of James Joyce
ISBN 978-3-89821-571-8

13   *Pablo Armellino*
Ob-scene Spaces in Australian Narrative
An Account of the Socio-topographic Construction of Space in Australian Literature
ISBN 978-3-89821-873-3

14   *Lance Weldy*
Seeking a Felicitous Space on the Frontier
The Progression of the Modern American Woman in O. E. Rölvaag, Laura Ingalls Wilder, and Willa Cather
ISBN 978-3-89821-535-0

15   *Rana Tekcan*
Too Far For Comfort
A Study on Biographical Distance
2nd, revised and expanded edition
ISBN 978-3-89821-995-2

16   *Paola Brusasco*
Writing Within/Without/About Sri Lanka
Discourses of Cartography, History and Translation in Selected Works by Michael Ondaatje and Carl Muller
ISBN 978-3-8382-0075-0

17   *Zeynep Z. Atayurt*
Excess and Embodiment in Contemporary Women's Writing
ISBN 978-3-89821-978-5

18   *Gianluca Delfino*
Time, History, and Philosophy in the Works of Wilson Harris
ISBN 978-3-8382-0265-5

19   *Taner Can*
Magical Realism in Postcolonial British Fiction: History, Nation, and Narration
ISBN 978-3-8382-0724-7

20   *Maria Festa*
History and Race in Caryl Phillips's *The Nature of Blood*
ISBN 978-3-8382-1433-7

Maria Festa

HISTORY AND RACE IN CARYL PHILLIPS'S *THE NATURE OF BLOOD*

Bibliografische Information der Deutschen Nationalbibliothek
Die Deutsche Nationalbibliothek verzeichnet diese Publikation in der Deutschen Nationalbibliografie; detaillierte bibliografische Daten sind im Internet über http://dnb.d-nb.de abrufbar.

Bibliographic information published by the Deutsche Nationalbibliothek
Die Deutsche Nationalbibliothek lists this publication in the Deutsche Nationalbibliografie; detailed bibliographic data are available in the Internet at http://dnb.d-nb.de.

Cover image: © Nirit Takele, 2020.

ISBN-13: 978-3-8382-1433-7
© *ibidem*-Verlag, Stuttgart 2020
Alle Rechte vorbehalten

Das Werk einschließlich aller seiner Teile ist urheberrechtlich geschützt. Jede Verwertung außerhalb der engen Grenzen des Urheberrechtsgesetzes ist ohne Zustimmung des Verlages unzulässig und strafbar. Dies gilt insbesondere für Vervielfältigungen, Übersetzungen, Mikroverfilmungen und elektronische Speicherformen sowie die Einspeicherung und Verarbeitung in elektronischen Systemen.

All rights reserved. No part of this publication may be reproduced, stored in or introduced into a retrieval system, or transmitted, in any form, or by any means (electronical, mechanical, photocopying, recording or otherwise) without the prior written permission of the publisher. Any person who does any unauthorized act in relation to this publication may be liable to criminal prosecution and civil claims for damages.

Printed in the EU

Contents

Acknowledgements

Introduction 1

1 *The Nature of Blood* 17

   1.1 The Author and His Novel 17

   1.2 "A passion for literature. Travelling furi- 27
       ously across borders and boundaries."

2 The Jewish Question 37

   2.1 Fragmented Narrative 37

      2.1.1 Stephan 38

      2.1.2 Eva 55

          2.1.2.1 Cyprus 55

          2.1.2.2 Bergen-Belsen 67

          2.1.2.3 London 77

      2.1.3 Malka 87

   2.2 The Jewish Question 92

3 Fragmented History 119

   3.1 The Disputable Concept of Race 119

   3.2 The Quasi-Othello 135

Appendix: A Conversation with Caryl Phillips 165

Works Cited 177

Acknowledgements

I am sincerely, profoundly grateful to Caryl Phillips as a writer but above all as a human being: his generosity, courtesy, attentiveness make him extraordinary.

I am deeply thankful to my professors. Their immense knowledge, their individual insights along with their thoughtful answers to my many questions have stimulated my intellectual curiosity and passion for Anglophone literatures: Roberto Beneduce, Carmen Concilio, Pietro Deandrea.

I would like to express my appreciation to the following scholars met during my writing process: Esterino Adami, Shaul Bassi, Ruth Anne Henderson, Françoise Kral, Clarinda Lawry, Bénédicte Ledent, John McLeod, Annalisa Oboe, Christopher Owen.

I also wish to thank all the people at *ibidem* Press who made this book possible and the artist whose work is featured on the front cover, Nirit Takele.

Special thanks to Patrizia Festa and her sisterly support; Roberta Graziano and her "Karen Walker" encouragement; Ulrike Voigt and her unwavering German-Canadian enthusiasm; Giulia Mascoli and our Phillipsian conversations; last but not least, Charles George Valente for his observations and comments on my writing and his unique friendship.

My love and gratitude to Grazia Palladino and Filippo Festa: my point of origin.

Maria Festa

Introduction

> Liverpool [...] It is disquieting to be in a place where history is so physically present, yet so glaringly absent from people's consciousness. But where is it any different? Maybe this is the modern condition.
> – Caryl Phillips (*Atlantic Sound* 93)

This study of Caryl Phillips's *The Nature of Blood* (1997) aims to provide a holistic reading of the multiple stories that are presented in the novel. This wide-canvas view of the seemingly disparate, disconnected threads in the text allows for underlying thematic and historical parallels to emerge and reveal themselves in ways that may not have seemed obvious on a first reading of the novel.

Phillips is one of the exponents of postcolonial and Black British literature. His commitment to his quest for identity and the feeling of belonging extends into other artistic fields such as theatre, radio, television, film, articles and essays. Phillips's refined, multifaceted erudition which emerges discreetly from all his work along with his varied interests and inquisitive mind stimulate readers' intellectual curiosity. In his autobiographical essay "A Life in Ten Chapters" from *Color Me English: Migration and Belonging Before and After 9/11*, Phillips, referring to his younger self as "the student," explains how an observant former teacher dissuaded him from pursuing a career in psychology:

> Dr Rabbitt informs the student that he has passed the first part of his degree in Psychology, Neurophysiology and Statics, but he reassures the student that at nineteen there is still time for him to reconsider his choice of a degree. Does he really wish to pursue psychology? The student patiently explains that he wishes to understand people, and that before university he was assiduously reading

Jung and Freud for pleasure. His unmoved tutor takes some snuff, and then he rubs his beard. So you want to know about people, do you? He patiently explains to the student that William James was the first professor of psychology at Harvard, but it was his brother, Henry, who really knew about people. The student looks at Dr Rabbitt, but he is unsure what to say. His tutor helps him to make the decision. 'Literature. If you want to know about people study English literature, not psychology.' (110-11)

Literature as a highly sophisticated laboratory for observing human nature can also be envisioned as a space where all sorts of disciplines intersect and where convergence, divergence as well as unexpected mixtures can occur. In this way, literature becomes a place of inquiry that encourages the development of ideas, reflections and investigations arising from our primordial attempt to understand the world we live in. In addition to this notion that literature reflects, absorbs and explores influences from a variety of fields, Phillips confers it the supplementary feature of social activism:

> As long as we have literature as a bulwark against intolerance, and as a force for a change, then we have a chance. [...] literature *is* plurality in action; it embraces and celebrates a place of no truths, it relishes ambiguity, and it deeply respects the place where everybody has the right to be understood. (*Color* 16; emphasis in the original)

The assertion that "literature *is* plurality in action" opens up and encapsulates an additional dimension of literature. The understanding of literature as a space for exploring ideas and human behaviour has been enlarged to include the belief that a novel, for instance, can also be an active "force for a change," for conceiving and making us realize a society without prejudice is possible. *The Nature of Blood*, even more so than any of Phillips's other artistic productions, epitomizes "the place where everybody has the right to be understood."

Phillips's deep political/humanist convictions are matched by a writing style and narrative choices that, without ever tilting into overstatement or self-conscious formal gymnastics, quietly challenge the reader to question some of the assumptions they may have about storytelling:

> I am not a novelist in the postmodern tradition who makes himself visible to the reader and orchestrates the narrative from the centre of the stage. I like to hide in the wings and turn the stage over to my characters. An occasional whispered prompt is all that I permit myself. (Phillips, "Fire" 177)

The Nature of Blood is no exception and Phillips does turn the stage over to his characters. They have democratic opportunities to reveal, introduce and provide details about themselves. The storytelling is delivered with an elaborate narrative structure in which individual stories are routinely interrupted only to be returned to later in the novel. Furthermore, the heterogeneous circumstances of the multiple stories resonate with one another, overlap or cross each other to form gradually recognisable emerging patterns and common traits. This complex framework develops, in readers, the habit of constant re-evaluating and reflecting on what came before (both narratively and historically). Perhaps as a gesture of empathy with his, at times, disoriented but inquisitive audience, Phillips offers occasional whispered prompts. These are incorporated in the narration in the form of encyclopaedic entries on the topics of suicide, the Jewish ghetto in Venice and his adaptation of Shakespeare's *Othello* (cf. 2.1.2.3; 2.2; 3.2.).

Phillips affirms that "in the case of *The Nature of Blood*, [he] was reasonably sure that the novel was going to be principally concerned with the Holocaust, but armed only with a general knowledge of the subject [he] felt that [he] had to become more familiar with history" ("Fire" 176). Phillips succeeded in "becom[ing] more familiar with history" to such an extent that Western history itself emerges as the central concern and focus of the narrative and the common denominator tying the heterogeneous accounts of events together. On another occasion Phillips goes into detail about his novel and seems to confirm the shift from a specific concern with the Holocaust to include events that pre-date as well as continue beyond the genocide perpetrated by Nazi Germany:

> The novel is, both directly and indirectly, about blood. About Europe's obsession with homogeneity, and her inability to deal with the heterogeneity that is – in fact – her natural condition. The practice of using blood as a barometer of acceptability is very deeply ingrained in the European consciousness [...] wherever one looks in European history, blood has been used as a pretext for the persecution of those whose faces do not fit on the canvas upon which the national portrait has been painted. ("Blood" 168-69)

In *The Nature of Blood* Phillips has broadened the scope of his exploration of his fragmented identity and permanent sense of "I feel at home here, but I don't belong. I am of, and not of, this place" (*New World Order* 4) to focus on the actor – Europe – that over the ages has played a crucial role in the economic and political structures of Western and non-Western societies. Furthermore, Phillips exposes the irony behind Europe's morality. He points his finger at Europe's "inability to deal with heterogeneity." He delves into history and cannot help but notice that the vital element held in common by members of the human race – blood – has been used as an instrument to legitimize exclusion and social injustices. This unavoidably has led to the creation of the figure of the Other: the individual or group arbitrarily assigned to a place at the bottom of the race/class hierarchy and tasked with enduring the greatest prejudice, exploitation, persecution in deeply unequal, stratified societies. Phillips with his Afro-Caribbean origins and British education examines the past of Europe, this continent that self-anointed itself the bearer of civilization and culture, as an alternative method of coming to terms with the issues of identity and sense of belonging. For the reasons given above and due to his acute awareness of British society's hesitant, limited acceptance of his place in a Western society, Phillips opted to write the novel in a non-European country in the hope of thus attaining distance and objectivity that would not otherwise have been possible:

> I can write in Europe, but my writing is always in danger from my environment. […] Bangkok is not Europe. […] Both culturally and physically, I have no connection to the country, or the people. I am a foreigner in the most radical sense, and this sense of alienation frees me to concentrate on my work. […] The novel I was working on is about Europe. It is a novel about the Holocaust. But not just this. The primary obsession was the Holocaust, which is – at least in my mind – related to my secondary obsession: race and faith as seen through the prism of sixteenth-century Venice. Othello's Venice; Shylock's Venice. To write this book I needed to be in Bangkok. I needed to be far away from Europe. ("Blood" 167-68)

It is interesting that just as Phillips felt he had to temporarily move to a modern non-European city to write about the European past, the novel he writes about the Holocaust in the nineteen-thirties and nineteen-forties is largely set centuries earlier or decades after the event in countries where extermination camps did not exist. It is as if only by stepping away from the time and place of the events of his "primary obsession" is he able to gain a wide enough perspective to fully understand them. The novel initially lets the story of the genocide of European Jews and other ethnic, social and political groups by the Nazis during World War II be told by its characters. Then, Phillips skilfully introduces other narrating voices, from Ethiopian Jews in Israel to sixteenth century Venice, and parallels with the Atlantic slave trade slowly begin to surface. It can be argued that Phillips's "primary obsession," even more than the murder of six million Jews in Nazi death camps, is the enduring fixation by a white, Euro-centric dominant class on some perceived Otherness attributed to different groups in its midst. In the late eighties, in the attempt to lessen "the tension between [himself] and [his] environment" (preface, *European Tribe* ix), Phillips travelled around Europe and "jotted various thoughts about a Europe [he] feel[s] both of and not of." He embarked on a journey into history rather than touring the natural, architectural and cultural sites that draw visitors to European countries. During his European travels he also visited Poland and the sites of the death camps:

> The next day Januesz drove me the thirty-five miles to Auschwitz. If there had been an airlink from Auschwitz to London, I would have taken it and flown home. In Auschwitz-Birkinau [Birkenau], the largest of the 5,000 camps, 4 million people were killed, 10,000 a day. The size of the figures was beyond my comprehension. At least the Atlantic slave trade had some vestige of logic, however unpalatable. Auschwitz transcended the imagination. (Phillips, "How much more" 97)

Upon his return to London, he "soon discovered that rather than solving the question of what Europe means to [him], the best [he] could hope for was that the experience might better define the parameters of

[his] 'problem'" (preface, *European Tribe* ix). To a certain extent, *The Nature of Blood* reflects his travel around Europe and his attempt to probe the intricacies of his "'problem.'" By delving into Western history Phillips is also looking into the roots of his fragmented identity.

In relation to his "secondary obsession: race and faith," Phillips ("Blood" 168) is drawn to the Jewish and African diasporas. Religion is at the core of the mass migration of the Jewish people after the period of Babylonian exile, whereas "race" – identified as difference in skin complexion – is at the core of the mass displacement of Africans as a consequence of the Atlantic slave trade. In *The Nature of Blood*, Phillips retraces the Jewish diaspora from fourteenth-century Colonia, Germany, where "Christian hysteria manifested itself in violence" (50) towards Jews until the nineteen-eighties. Phillips alludes to the two diasporas through the stories of his immigrant African characters and through the similarities that become subtly but undeniably apparent to the reader between the two major displacements of human populations in Western history.

The peculiarity and intricacy of the narrative challenge readers' knowledge of the events described. The diverse narrative strands and settings in the novel allow for, maybe even invite, different interpretations. However, in order to investigate the complex, multi-layered events portrayed in *The Nature of Blood*, I have opted to focus on the historical dimension of the novel. With this in mind, I have singled out four characters – Stephan, Eva, Malka and the African General – whose individual lives are traversed and deeply affected by extraordinary historical circumstances. This selection helped scaffold my reading of the novel, as well as of history, but most importantly, it provided a clear direction in my research.

This study has been divided into three parts plus an appendix that contains a conversation with the author that occurred in Caen, France, in May 2017. The first part introduces the author, his work, his characteristic writing style, his approach to literature and his alternative understanding of history as far as is required for the purposes of this study.

The second part analyses the characters of Stephan, Eva and Malka, and the last section deals with the Jewish question. I argue that Stephan's narrative operates as a frame, while his character functions as a narrative hub in the text. The frame can be interpreted as a closed border that contains the fragmented stories; the hub can be viewed as the focal point through which the fragmented stories pass. If we adhere to Phillips's understanding of history as a non-linear record of events, Stephan becomes a point of convergence from where multiple connections among historical events radiate. Stephan is also a thematic hub, an entry point to a discussion on Zionism, the subsequent comparison with Pan-Africanism as well as the British political involvement in Palestine. Historical data and perspectives are based on Alan Hart's *Zionism*; Stephen Howe's *Afrocentrism*; the conversation "Pan-African Legacies, Afropolitan Futures" between Joseph-Achille Mbembe and Sarah Balakrishnan.

The second character, Eva, personifies the violence inflicted on Jews by the Holocaust. Her fragmented, bewildered narration shows her deeply traumatized state of mind. Her vivid accounts of events along with the omniscient narrator's reports that fill the gaps in Eva's reminiscences portray the atrocious persecution of European Jews by the Nazis. My analysis of Eva follows the locations where the events occur: Cyprus, Bergen-Belsen and London. Cyprus is the first setting of the novel. In the aftermath of World War II, the Mediterranean island replicates the reality of another form of confinement. Due to British policies in regard to the settlement of Jews in Palestine, the survivors of the Nazi death camps are enclosed in British detention camps before boarding the ships that will take them to the "promised land." Giorgio Agamben's study of concentration camps and the inclusion-exclusion relationships that occur in this particular context constitutes the basis for my comparison between German and British camps and my attempt to provide Eva with, in Phillips's words, "the right to be understood" ("Color" 16). Ironically, Eva's silence and need to be alone is respected and met with examples of empathy while she is detained in Cyprus, something which does not happen when she arrives, as a free person, in London. I rely on trauma studies to try to interpret Eva's behaviour and thoughts, specifically on Sigmund Freud and his first theories of recovery from trauma, along with current theorists such as Judith Lewis Herman and Sophia Richman who promote the practice of the autobiographical process. As is the case for Eva, this practice allows the individual to go through his/her past experience privately and in any moment that feels safe for this kind of unpleasant examination of painful experiences. Through her soliloquies, Eva provides details about her *persona*, simultaneously attempting to come to terms with her traumatic experience and regain a sense of continuity and wholeness. The section devoted to Bergen-Belsen deals with the shocking reality of the death camp. Eva manages to depict her life before and during her confinement, even though her fragmented thoughts sometimes appear, on first reading, random and elliptical. Nonetheless, the omniscient narrator's voice takes over every time the character seems unable to describe details or feelings that are likely to deepen her profound psychological wound. The omniscient narrator's voice, for instance, meticulously describes "the process of gassing" (176) when Eva, whom we learn "burn[s] bodies" (107), remains silent about her forced membership to a *Sonderkommando* aiding with the disposal of gas chamber victims.

Zygmunt Bauman and Elias Canetti provide valuable insights into the ideology and practice of the Nazis in their goal of creating a *judenfrei* Germany. Bauman puts forth the argument that the Holocaust was a product, rather than an aberration, of a highly regulated, stratified civilization.[1] Canetti illustrates the survivor's sense of shame and guilt

---

[1] Joseph-Achille Mbembe in his essay "Necropolitics" offers a further consideration on the matter. He starts with the assumption that colonial imperialism is at the origin of Nazi extermination camps whereas the systematic, industrialized procedure of putting Jews to death is a consequence of technological development that allowed the In-

along with the importance for the individual of being addressed by name. Their argumentation contributed to better comprehending Eva's reminiscences, and revealed stimulating new perspectives on a topic which European readers might feel they were already quite familiar with.

The last location, London, manifests itself as an unwelcoming city, although Eva envisions it as home. The words employed by Eva to describe the London taxi driver's unfriendly manners at the end of the ride echo the feeling of rejection experienced by the former colonized people who felt they belonged, as children of the British Empire, to their "mother country" and consequently expected to be accepted as "one of [their] own kind" (65).

In *The Nature of Blood* Phillips is working on a wide canvas. When he introduces the character of Malka he is expanding the narrative to include a non-European voice with a very different history who is both a foil and a complement to Eva and Stephan and their stories. The novel is characterised by reverse as well as parallel narratives. Similarly to Eva, Malka's thoughts are presented in the form of interior monologues. Unlike Eva, she is in her thirties and, as stated by Stephan, "belong[s] to another place" (210) – Ethiopia –. With Phillips's "secondary obsession: race and faith" ("Blood" 168) in mind, it is possible to make the case that Malka embodies the Jewish and African diaspora. In some ways the novel can be compared to a photographic film, or even to a developed print film along with its respective transparent negatives. In this analogy, Malka and Eva represent the complementary, barely distinguishable black and white images while Western history stands for the developed colour print film. Phillips appears to be saying something similar when he comments that "the canvas upon which the national portrait has been painted" has

---

dustrial Revolution and continuing to advance made World War I the first global war and one of the largest wars until that time in Western history. The gas chamber is a product of what Mbembe defines as "the serialization of technical mechanisms" and "having become mechanized, serialized execution was transformed into a purely technical, impersonal, silent, and rapid procedure" ("Necropolitics" 18).

omitted faces like Malka and Eva's – "faces [that] do not fit on." – ("Blood" 169)

The utopic assumption that a shared religion overcomes differences in skin colour and origin is disputed by the treatment of Ethiopian Jews in the "promised land" and leads to the last section of the second part: the Jewish question. I begin by exploring the notion of home and the meaning attached to it by diasporic people. I also investigate the figure of the "Other," relying extensively on Toni Morrison's lectures to reveal connections between the various stories in *The Nature of Blood*. "Otherness" in Phillips's novel is an indication of perceived cultural and physical differences that invariably lead to hierarchies of power, to superior-inferior / master-servant relationships and inevitably to abuse of power by dominant groups. When Phillips juxtaposes German-Jewish Eva's story with Ethiopian-Israeli Malka's situation, with all their intersecting elements of displacement, discrimination, gender, class and ethnicity, readers are confronted with the inadequacy of simplistic, Eurocentric readings of history. Bénédicte Ledent, a major influence on the present study, declares that "*The Nature of Blood* constantly obliges the reader to find his/her way around a maze-like text" (*Caryl Phillips* 136). This disruption, in which uncritically held assumptions of history are eroded, is intentional. The character of Malka, whose story in some ways supplies a key that can potentially open the door out of the confining maze, constitutes Phillips' "final piece of [...] the puzzle" ("Blood" 168) that lets readers complete the larger picture connecting Jewish and African forced migrations. Malka exposes the limitations inherent in Stephan's ambitious, idealistic project to create a prejudice-free homeland for "Jews of all ages and backgrounds" (73). Her arrival in Israel is the result of an altruistic plan by the Jewish state for re-uniting the white and black siblings of Israel. In reality, the "promised land" becomes yet another example of the dominant white society that replicates the superior-inferior racist view towards its darker-skinned citizens evident in European colonies in Africa. Similar to the British Empire, which defined itself as the "bearer of culture and civilization" to its colonies and settlements, Israel immediately sets to re-educate its newcomers who have been uprooted from their African villages in the language and Westernized ways of the country's European settlers. However, instead of being included in the new, large, multicultural society, Ethiopian Jews are excluded from "the canvas upon which the national portrait has been painted" ("Blood" 169) and relegated to *the edge of the city*" (207; emphasis in the original). The words employed by Malka to criticize the unrealized promise of unity and inclusion under one common religion in the "promised land" echo the feeling of rejection experienced by formerly colonised people who imagined they would be coming home to their "mother country" and subsequently discovered they were clearly not considered "one of [the host country's] own kind" (65).

To gain a wider view on the issue of religion, I explore Judaism under the perspective of Freud's study on *Moses and Monotheism*. Freud's research provides an explanation of the reasons that triggered hate and persecution of the Jews from the origins of Judaism as a monotheistic religion. In this maze-like novel, "The Most Serene Republic of Venice" (48) allows readers to start noticing some of the thematic lines that will connect the various narratives that make up *The Nature of Blood*. Phillips delves into his "secondary obsession: race and faith [...] through the prism of sixteenth-century Venice. Othello's Venice; Shylock's Venice" ("Blood" 168). At a certain point in the novel, one of the narrating voices summarizes the prosecution lawyer's version of the lead up to the alleged murder of a Christian child for Passover celebrations:

> Everything began on a day in September during the previous year, when the Jews were celebrating a holiday known as the Feast of the Tabernacles. [...] 'You know that, before Easter, we will need a little Christian blood for our bread. My friend,

produce a young child, for you know how to do it, and in return I will give you ten ducati in cash.' (100)

As illustrated in section 2.2, the three indicted Jews are tried before being found guilty and sentenced to death. These trials resemble the Venetian court of justice in Shakespeare's *The Merchant of Venice* (1596-1599). According to the local law, Shylock's insistence that he be repaid, as previously agreed, by "just a pound of flesh" (*Merchant* 4.1) is considered an attempt on a Venetian citizen's life. He is punished with the loss of "one half his goods, the other half / Comes to the privy coffer of the state, / And the offender's life lies in the mercy / Of the Duke only." In Shakespeare's play characters exhibit complex, multi-layered motives and it would be a mistake to reduce the play to a single interpretation. Nevertheless, *The Merchant of Venice* does depict legal and political Christian dominance over a Jewish minority grounded in prejudice and racist myths of Jewish cupidity and cruelty. This is evident in the verdict reached: Shylock is exempted from the penalties on the condition that he "presently become a Christian" (*Merchant* 4.1). This option is not available to the falsely accused Jews in *The Nature of Blood*, nor are they, unlike Shylock, given the opportunity to express themselves in court. Their public execution eerily replicates the crimes committed against Jews during the Second World War:

> The condemned were attached by means of a long chain to iron stakes on the scaffolding, and then the torch holders lit their torches and immediately ignited the woodpiles. [...] the flames enveloped everything, and one could see only fire. As the blaze consumed flesh and blood, the spectators, on both land and water, were deeply moved by the power of the Christian faith and its official Venetian guardians. (154-55)

The third part looks at the African General in the Venice section of the novel as well as the importance of challenging conventional, linear versions of history. I explore how the murky concept of race has been used to justify particular groups' self-defined superior status over other groups' status and the figure of the African-born leader of the Venetian army perfectly incarnates the paradoxes of the relationship between subjugator and subjugated.

In the first section, Ivan Hannaford, Michael Banton and Jonathan Harwood have been valuable sources in my intent to trace the origin of prejudice based on visible physical differences which are labelled under the term of "race." The historical *excursus* leads to the employment of this disputable concept in the modern context. I illustrate different views on the issue as put forth by Paul Gilroy, Stuart Hall, Hannah Arendt, Shaul Bassi, Harold Cyril Bibby. Their reflections and conclusions all suggest that the common denominator in every case is the use of race to signify the "Other" as the vulnerable individual who, for different reasons, becomes the target for exploitation and/or persecution.

In section 3.2, I analyze the figure of the African General. The experienced military leader in the service of the Republic of Venice wields considerable power and yet feels helpless and vulnerable. He longs to integrate but is rebuffed by the city that has requested his talents. The African General is the outcast who constantly deals with the antithetical feelings of belonging-longing, inclusion-exclusion, superior-inferior. His narrating voice never states his name. Nonetheless, readers may easily recognize a strong resemblance with the main character in Shakespeare's *Othello*, a hypothesis that is confirmed later by Phillips's "occasional whispered prompt" ("Fire" 177). I compare the two texts but emphasize Phillips's revisiting of the story with a view to making a fresh appraisal. The quasi-Othello (whom Bénédicte Ledent [136] calls "the Othello-like character") is one of the victims of Western history but he eventually vindicates himself as a human being who, in some ways, would be justified in considering himself superior to his Venetian overlords. Furthermore, the African General's story represents a fertile ground for postcolonial researchers. The quasi-Othello's day-to-day reality in Venice draws our attention to issues of whiteness, privilege, slavery, exclusion and the longing for acceptance, issues that numerous intellectuals and scholars have studied extensively. In this section I rely on Frantz Fanon, Jacques Lacan, Homi K. Bhabha, Robert J. C. Young, Pietro Deandrea.

Stephen Clingman discusses Phillips's concern with identity and suggests that Phillips's life is "like a segment of the map of the twentieth-century migrancy with all its vulnerabilities and juxtapositions" (144). It may be argued that some of those "vulnerabilities and juxtapositions," such as the systematic subjugation of ethnic groups on the grounds of prejudice, and the quest for home are at the heart of virtually all the stories in *The Nature of Blood*. The novel also gives form to the author's attitude towards the narrow focus and inherent biases that riddle traditional accounts of Western history that most pupils learn in European schools. Phillips suggests that literature, with its potentially more inclusive scope and its freedom from the chronological, linear storytelling conventions that define most history books, offers a vital tool for bridging the gaps in the mainstream Europeans' knowledge of Western history:

> I had learnt that in a situation in which history is distorted, the literature of a people often becomes its history, its writers the keepers of the past, present, and future. In this situation a writer can infuse a people with a sense of their own unique identity and spiritually kindle the fire of resistance ("How much more" 99).

The marginalized conditions and the disconnected fragments recounted in the novel simultaneously underscore the fact that our history is incomplete (because it has not included the voice of the displaced, of the non-white) and challenge readers to cross "borders and boundaries" (introduction, *New World Order* 5) to engage with these very human voices. On a formal level, the novel's disjointed stream of consciousness narrative can be read as an attempt to address this absence of the "Other" from our history. On an intellectual level, the novel reflects Phillips's conviction that to write fiction is to partake in a transformative social and political process that aims to make cultures more inclusive and humane. For Phillips, "literature *is* plurality in action" ("Color" 16).

1 *The Nature of Blood*

1.1 The Author and His Novel

Caryl Phillips was born on the Caribbean island of Saint Kitts, grew up in Leeds, England, and currently lives in the U.S. where he holds the chair of Professor of English at Yale University. Phillips's copious publications include novels, essays, anthologies, theatre, television, and radio plays as well as a number of screenplays. The frequent experience of moving from one place to another has been a constant reality from the author's earliest age and has continued into his adulthood. He has taught at universities in Ghana, Sweden, Singapore, Barbados, India, Canada and the United States, in addition to his sojourning as visiting professor at universities in Europe and North America. He also often travels as a tourist and accounts of these trips are published in Phillips's collections of essays.[1]

In 2016, the Nigerian-American writer and photographer Teju Cole published his first collection of photographs. One of them, taken in September 2014 shows a shop window in Zurich, with earth globes on shelves, and for each globe the visible side is set on a different location (Cole 140). At a first glance, these globes induce me to look for places that are familiar to my eye and mind. At the same time, the vision of different locations, side by side on a shelf, evokes a mental image of a restless writer, who, from a phenomenological perspective, through the act of writing, attempts to ascertain his/her origin and locate himself/herself among the things of the world. In the solitary moment devoted to writing, the individual engages himself/herself in a personal reflexive self-examination process, and in this kind of analysis the individual aims for a better understanding of his/her life.

Cole's photograph could be used to illustrate the restless, multifaceted aspect of Phillips's writing and life. Arguably, Phillips's

---

[1] The biographical information provided here comes from Caryl Phillips's official website.

above-mentioned experiences have shaped an individual with a persistent desire for change, action, or merely finding his origin, and in my mind this idea of Phillips moving from one place to another on a regular basis has found its material expression in that photograph taken by Cole. My interpretation of this photograph seems to be supported by Phillips's words from the preface of his selected essays, *A New World Order*, in which he describes a realization he had in Leeds: "I am seven years old in the north of England; too late to be coloured, but too soon to be British. I recognize the place, I feel at home here, but I don't belong. I am of, and not of, this place" (4). This experience recurs when he travels Africa, St. Kitts and the United States. Phillips continues by blaming the random lottery of history for his feeling of not belonging to the place called home:

> History dealt me four cards; an ambiguous hand.
> A life lived along the twin rails of reading and writing. The one act informing the other. And all the while a particular interest in the work of those who have been dealt the same ambiguous hand. Who am I? How do I explain who I am? How do I come to be here? (4-5)

Phillips realizes that history dealt Frantz Fanon, Ignatius Sancho, James Baldwin and John Coetzee the same ambiguous hand. Consequently, his particular interest in their work induces him to explore their reflections and thoughts:

> All of them writing about their condition. Reading about their condition and then writing about my own. Developing a passion for literature. Developing a passion for transgression. A confused fifteen-year old boy is confronted with the reality of Anne Frank and realises that he is not alone. He begins to recognise the laborious certainties of the old order. A life lived along the twin rails

of reading and writing. The one informing the other. A passion for literature. Travelling furiously across borders and boundaries. (5)

Phillips seems to perceive literature as the key to knowledge and self-discovery along with the opportunity to move freely and boldly through time (history) and space in the attempt to establish his own origin and consequently to locate himself among the things of the world.

Roland Barthes provides a definition of literature from a semiotic perspective: "literature is essentially an activity of language" as well as "an *institutional* use of language" (qtd. in Rylance 9-10; author's emphasis). Barthes moreover suggests that the use of language generates the writer's personal style, and that the process of phrasing originates in the writer's body and past and gradually becomes the very reflexes of his/her art. A writer's personal style is in large part not an intentional result, but rather a spontaneous offshoot of personal experience, preferences, cultural/historical context which connects the writer to his/her society (Barthes, *Grado zero* 10). According to Barthes the process of phrasing originates in the body of the writer. Similarly, Enzo Paci defines the act of writing thus: "there is no such thing as the word detached from the body. The written word does not exist: when we read it, we trace it back to its original incarnation, or to ourselves, if we are not able to imagine the living person who wrote it. The disembodied word, if it were possible, would not make sense" (translation mine).[2] Both statements can be applied to Phillips's writing. This introspective consideration may also aim at putting together the pieces of his own fragmented identity.

---

[2] "La parola distaccata dal corpo non esiste. Non esiste la parola scritta: leggendo la riconduciamo alla sua originaria incarnazione, alla nostra, se non riusciamo a immaginare la persona viva che l'ha scritta. La parola disincarnata, se fosse possibile, non avrebbe senso" (22-23).

Phillips's novels epitomize what is defined as post-colonial literature. His narrative is characterized by the tensions between belonging and exclusion; between strangeness and familiarity; between arrival and departure; between migration and settlement. His exploration of slavery helps shed light on the contemporary migrant condition and feelings of dislocation and rootlessness are a central concern in his novels. Phillips's vision of diaspora is grounded in the material inequalities, and lived experiences of race, racism, and multi-culturalism, and underscore his commitment to acknowledging the nuances of identity and identification. Furthermore, Phillips's novels challenge the reader by presenting him or her with discontinuous narrations, fragmented accounts of events and multiple perspectives, as if to suggest a fragmented identity evident both in his characters and in himself. Phillips is elusive in describing his fictional characters. However, in every novel, the multitude of personalities which participate in the narration are in some unspecified way related to each other. The connections are not made explicit by the author and it is always up to reader to establish them. Moreover, the reader deals with multilayered characters and the associations/relations become clearer as the novel arrives at its final pages or after a further reading of the text. Phillips's writing style is refined, I would even say lyrical, and marked by a high register. It can be regarded as a cross between narrative and poetry.

I am of the opinion that, up to the present moment, *The Nature of Blood* is Phillips's most elaborate and challenging novel. The narration is not organized into chapters: it is an aggregate of historical occurrences and situations that occur over a large span of time between the fifteenth and the twentieth century where themes, characters, and incidents resonate against one another. Phillips explores notions of race and identity by drawing indirect parallels between the experiences of African victims of the trans-Atlantic slave trade and that of European Jews deported to German concentration camps; between pan-African nationalism and Zionism. His reflections shift from Africa, which was at the centre of the European colonial expansion and the slave trade, to Europe, where the prejudice against Jews has its origin, persisted across the centuries and culminated in the murderous master race ideology of the German Nazis.

The fragmented narrative flow in *The Nature of Blood* and the resulting gaps challenge readers' knowledge of history. The missing pieces in the story (and in history) require readers to fill in the empty spaces through the tools available to them, such as memory, mental association or human empathy and thus participate in a new understanding of history.

The narrating voice is also fragmented. *The Nature of Blood* does not contain a table of contents either.[3] Upon opening of the book, readers do not receive information about the structure of the narration, or hints on the plot. Instead, characters are granted introductory presentations that are marked by an identical first person singular narrating voice. This voice first provides general details about the personage, to switch then progressively to a proper presentation conveying the character's name, age (sometimes), and place of origin. At a first reading, the novel may appear as a disjointed stream of consciousness: the thoughts and feelings of the characters are presented as they occur and leave us wondering who is talking, when the action is taking place, if the different events are related to each other.

In the following, four fictional characters, whose alternating and interwoven narratives make up a non-linear history, will be introduced in order to describe the historical fragments featuring in the novel.

These four characters appear here in the order in which they are presented in the novel. At the very beginning of the narration, we listen to a conversation:

---

[3] Actually, the lack of a table of contents is pervasive in Phillips's novels, exceptions to this being *The Lost Child* (2015) and *A View of the Empire at Sunset* (2018). This fact requires a real commitment from his readers. What might appear at first confusing and, perhaps, non-sensical, acquires meaning over the course of the narration and definitively as soon as the reading of the novel is completed.

'Tell me, what will be the name of the country?'
'Our country', I said. 'The country will belong to you too.'
The boy looked down at the sand, then scratched a short nervous line with his big toe.
'Tell me, what will be the name of our country?'
I paused for a moment, in the hope that he might relax. And then I whispered, as though confessing something to him.
'Israel. Our country will be called Israel.'(3)

The dialogue between the "I" and "the boy" allows us to infer one of the topics of the novel. Only a few lines later, we can deduce the precise time and location, that is to say, shortly after the Second World War, when "the British had initiated their policy of turning away refugee ships from Palestine, and off-loading the passengers on to their island of Cyprus" (5). One of the speakers above is Stephan Stern, who before the outbreak of the war "had journeyed to the British colony of Palestine, for he wanted to defend the new Jewish settlement against attacks from the Arabs, and to prepare the land for large-scale settlement by Jews of all ages and backgrounds" (73). At the end of the novel, and hence later in time, we become aware that Stephan lives somewhere in the state of Israel. In the last pages he shares his thoughts with the reader. He recalls pre-war memories of his young wife and their daughter, both left in the United States as he joined the underground army with the intent to regain the "promised land" (73) for his people. He also thinks of his brother when he visits him before permanently leaving Germany along with an afternoon spent outdoors with his young nieces, who are unable to interact with him, and "left him alone on the bench, his arms outstretched, reaching across the years" (212). This image of Stephan with his arms wide open to the flowing of time gives the impression of an individual open to life, even though he is in a static position. Despite his apparent physical stillness, he is, at this point of the novel, actually making final preparations to "travel [...] furiously across borders and boundaries," very much in the way Phillips the novelist does in his texts and in the act of writing.[4]

The voids in Stephan Stern's fragmented story are filled in by the narratives of other characters whose first person singular voices interrupt and take over the narrative to introduce us to their stories. The following thoughts allow us to locate the second selected character:

> I WATCH as the trucks come roaring into the camp, dust and mud flying up behind their wheels. As the men jump down to the ground, they whistle and shout to each other. Then silence descends over them. They shield their eyes and look about themselves in disbelief. Silence. [...] The men are standing and staring at us. [...] This silent scene of us facing them. Skeletons facing men. Former prisoners facing liberators. [...] We are free. These English men have arrived on this warm spring day and now we are free. [...] I tilt my face so that I might soak up what little sun there is. I have no strength to be happy. My thin bones would shake and fall apart were they to be subjected to such an emotion. (12-13)

The talk of prisoners and of thin bones that would shake and fall apart suggests a survivor of the Nazi concentration camps. As previously mentioned by Stephan, we are able to locate the setting when the narrating voice identifies the liberators: "these English men have arrived

---

[4] This apparent paradox between staying in one place and simultaneously moving across time and geography, reminds of Leopold Bloom in James Joyce's *Ulysses* (1922). The employment of the adverb "furiously" unites Phillips and Stephan (along with Leopold Bloom), whose wandering in history is marked by intensity, passion and a sense of urgency. In their quest for knowledge their thoughts, reflections and sometimes actions, cross physical and political edges/frontiers and aim at a better understanding of their own lives as well as the lived world.

[...] and now we are free," implying once again the island of Cyprus. The identity of the character emerges slowly through reminiscences of life before the mass deportation of Jews: "Mama married beneath her. [...] Her husband was a well-respected man, a young doctor, who eventually provided her with a beautiful four-storey house and two daughters" (14). Later we are told: "My name is Eva Stern. I am twenty-one years old" (35). The family name "Stern" establishes a relationship between these two first person voices we meet at the beginning of the novel, and a few lines later, Eva confirms this familial bond: "Uncle Stephan was Papa's only brother" (72).

The next first person singular voice, that is to say, the third one selected for this section, takes us back in time:

> I arrived in the spring and was immediately enchanted by this city-state. I approached by water and found myself propelled by the swift tides across the lonely empty spaces of the forbidding lagoon. [...] What ingenuity! Nothing in my native country had prepared me for the splendour of the canals, but it was not only these waterways which seized my attention. The magnificence of the buildings that lined the canals overwhelmed my senses, and upon the grandest of these buildings, proud images of the Venetian lion were carved in wood, chiselled in stone, or wrought in iron. (106-07)

The "city-state" is a clear reference to the Republic of Venice whose "proud images of the Venetian lion" emphasize its status as a leading European economic, trading and maritime power during the Middle Ages and the Renaissance. After this preliminary statement, the character asserts:

> I had moved from the edge of the world to the centre. [...] I, a man born of royal blood, a mighty warrior, yet a

man who, at one time, could view himself only as a poor slave, had been summoned to serve this state; to lead the Venetian army; to stand at the very centre of the empire. (107)

In the above passage, "from the edge of the world to the centre" and "the very centre of the empire" could easily be a reference to the British Empire, or almost any other imperial power for that matter, and reminds us of the relationship between the colonizer and the colonized. The character's previous experience of living as "a poor slave" further underscores his status as an outsider who, eventually, finds himself residing in the "centre of the empire."

As mentioned earlier, in the last pages of the novel, we listen to Stephan's voice describing his life in Israel, and in this new setting we come across another first person singular voice, our fourth selected character:

(Together with my parents and my brother and sister. (In our village, nobody had ever seen a light bulb or a telephone. Of course we were unprepared.) We lived as farmers and weavers. [...] At dawn, we discovered that we were travelling through a desert that was littered with the skeletons of camels and goats. [...] And then on to the embassy compound [...] And from the embassy to the airport. We just let it happen. [...]) (199; emphasis in the original)

Desert, camels and airport suggest the forced mass migration of Ethiopian Jews to Israel in the eighties:

My sister and I wondered, in this new land, would our babies be born white? We, the people of the House of Israel, we were going home. No more wandering. No long-

> *er landless. No more tilling of soil that did not belong to us. What is your name? Malka.* (201; emphasis in the original)

Malka is a young Ethiopian Jewish woman. She has a brief encounter with Stephan, and her migrant experience in the "House of Israel" resembles, to a certain degree, the experience of former colonized individuals arriving in the so-called mother country after the Second World War, specifically the experience of the "Windrush generation." The name derives from the ship – the Empire Windrush – that, in 1948, brought one of the first groups of West Indians to Britain to address labour shortages; despite being needed, they faced racism and discrimination:[5]

> *First we will teach you the language, then when you leave the absorption centre you will be able to study at the university. Don't worry, your parents will find work. […] And yes, I went to your university – I am a nurse – but I cannot find a job.* (207; emphasis in the original)

The fictional characters described above can serve as a sort of table of contents for the novel and should help readers better identify individuals and events and lend the narrative a more approachable and cohesive order.

---

[5] This sense of belonging but feeling unwanted is also described in novels from the Black British Literature. *The Lonely Londoners* (1956) by Samuel Selvon and *Small Island* (2004) by Andrea Levy, for instance, portray the Caribbean immigrant experience in the unfriendly and unwelcoming mother country.

1.2 "A passion for literature. Travelling furiously across borders and boundaries."[6]

"History, Stephen said, is a nightmare from which I am trying to awake."
– James Joyce (*Ulysses* 34)

From the moment we are born, our life is projected into the future. For the majority of us the concept of the past is relegated to the realm "no longer current, over." This "no longer current" dimension of our lives is what we refer to as history. Most people regard history as a subject taught in schools; consisting of collections of facts to be learned by heart and eventually to be stored in our short-term memory. Hence, history seems to be only a series of events, dates, and names.

According to the Oxford Dictionary, history is "a continuous, typically chronological, record of events" ("History"). It is characterized by a sense of continuity and the resulting possibility of tracing events on a time-line is familiar to most Westerners. Nevertheless, this view of history and of the past is not universally accepted. Barthes, for instance, questions the authority of history and compares it to a divider between the past and the present when he rhetorically asks: "Is History not simply that time when we were not born?" (*Camera Lucida* 64). Phillips subscribes to a similar definition of history and goes further by suggesting that History is also the past of each individual's own life. As a matter of fact, in his novels, he relates life experiences from different times and locations to his readers. Arguably, the subject taught in school and soon forgotten as human beings project their lives into the future is considered by Phillips as an aggregation of individuals' pasts with the larger History as background. Phillips's particular writing style characterized by gaps in the narrative mirrors this idea of History as a receptacle rather than a time-line. In this way Phillips invites his readers to question their knowledge of main historical events

---

[6] Phillips, *New World Order* 5.

and "to travel furiously across borders and boundaries" (New *World* 5).

In *The Nature of Blood* the diversity of alternating (mostly) first person narrating voices provides a fresh perception of History. For instance, the interwoven narratives of Stephan, Eva, the African General and Malka stand for a non-linear pattern of past events and emphasize the tendency of a tragic set of circumstances to occur. However, despite the importance of these characters and their individual stories, in this study, I put forth the idea that the past and the essentially non-linear nature of History prove to be the main character in *The Nature of Blood*, and the four individual stories serve to underline the reiteration of specific historical events.

Our first character, Stephan, is a Jewish activist who dedicates his life to the "House of Israel" (201). His first person singular voice frames the narration of the novel. His quest for the promised land offers the possibility to draw a parallel with Pan-Africanism: an intellectual movement for a unified nation where all people of the African diaspora can live. With the coming of independence for many African countries in the decades following World War II, the cause of African unity lost some of its appeal with the newly independent nations whose political leaders were not well-disposed towards a supranational government and resulting restrictions to their own political power. Over a century after the First Pan African Conference that was held in 1900 in London, England, the quest for a united voice as a way of resisting any form of imperialism and colonialism and of giving rise to a unified African identity and culture still seems to be a distant target (Kinni 54).

Through the years, disagreements in implementing the original set of principles and beliefs have led to divisions in the Zionist movement and a number of separate strands have emerged (Qresel 171). Both, Pan-Africanism and Zionism, seem to be doomed to failure. Once again history denies equality, freedom and justice to peoples who bear the stigma of diaspora.

The second character, Eva, is a Jewish survivor from the Nazi concentration camps. During her internment she belonged to a *Sonderkommando*. She escapes death in the camp only to later commit suicide in London. Like many before her, Eva is a victim of the ethnic violence recurring in European history. The prejudice against Jews is deeply-rooted in Europe (the first documented instance stemming from England in 1144) (Bassi, *Essere* 111), and Phillips illustrates it in the novel:

> The Jews had first begun journeying to Portobuffole in 1424, many of them migrating from Colonia in Germany. Back in 1349, the Christian people of that region had suddenly become incensed and irrational from fear of the plague, and the Jews began to suffer as this Christian hysteria manifested itself in violence. Eventually the Jews could take no more and they barricaded themselves into their large synagogue, set fire to it, and recited moribund prayers to each other as they waited for the end. The few Jews that survived this catastrophe remained in the region, but finally they were driven out. [...] In 1424, the Jews of Colonia were finally expelled for good, and most decided to travel to the Republic of Venice, where it was rumoured that life was more secure. (50-51)

Twentieth century London is to post-Second-World-War Europe what the perceived safety of fifteenth century Venice represented to German Jews fleeing persecution four hundred years earlier. According to Niall Ferguson's study on the history of the British Empire, starting from the end of the sixteenth until the twentieth century, London embodied, in the mind of those who lived at the outer edges of the Empire, the ideals of home, equality, freedom, and justice. London was envisioned as home, and the right place for a new beginning after the Second World War. Phillips emphasizes this through the character of

Eva, who goes to London with the intent of making "a new life together" (188) with Gerry, the British soldier she met in Cyprus. Ferguson (15) also argues that the end of the Second World War officially marks the beginning of the fall of the British Empire which culminates in the nineteen-sixties, even though the reverberations of decolonization are still palpable today.

In addition to the factual information it provides, the passage above also reminds us of the recurring pattern of History, of how events have a tendency to repeat themselves in other completely different historical periods. In the nineteen-thirties Europe witnessed the rise of German totalitarianism and what Ferguson (15) defines as Hitler's "Empire of the Evil." The crimes committed against Jews during the Second World War eerily replicate the public execution of the falsely accused Servadio, Moses and Giacobbe in fifteenth century Venice: "Today, they continue to burn bodies. (I burn bodies.) Burning bodies. First, she lights the fire. Pour gasoline, make a torch, and then ignite the pyre. Wait for the explosion as the fire catches, and then wait for the smoke" (170). This memory, resembling an instruction manual checklist, belongs to Eva. She informs us of her traumatic life experience in the Nazi concentration camp. In the passage, the verb "to continue" along with the repetition of "burn bodies" strengthened by alliteration, suggests a procedure through which death, for a *Sonderkommando* member, becomes "routine" (168).

The third character, the African General, another survivor of wars and an outsider, brings us back in time. Even though he never states his name, the words with which he describes himself establish a clear reference to Shakespeare's Othello, which is then confirmed by an inserted informative note on the Bard's play. As in Shakespeare's tragedy, Phillips's character is a Moorish general who has to lead the Venetian army against Turks in the island of Cyprus.

A parallel is drawn between the Jewish combatant Stephan and the African General in the following two passages. About Stephen it is said that he imagined his own child growing up without ever knowing her father. It turned out that his wife had written to him and informed him that she understood from his silence that he preferred Arabs to his own child. To her mind, the serious responsibilities of family were incompatible with the responsibilities of this self-proclaimed new life of his. (77)

Similarly, the African General casts his "mind back to the wife and child" he had "left behind in [his] native country [...] As was the custom with a warrior, there had been no formal marriage, it being understood that at any moment [he] might lose [his] life" (134). Both characters embrace a cause that requires commitment but implies loneliness. Both characters feel like *personae non gratae* at the centre of the Empire.

Stephan remembers his life in Germany during the rise of Nazism and how freedom to Jewish citizens was at first restricted and then denied: "Desks were rearranged. We now had to sit at the back, near the door. Soon after there were young men in new strange uniforms. Saluting each other. Bright new flags. [...] Ernst, our lives are getting smaller. Shops and businesses are closing. You must go" (10).

Similarly, the African General is a warrior who feels like a foreigner and inferior among Venetians, a conviction that is underscored by the often repeated sentence "I was clearly not one of their own" (129).

Phillips's re-telling of *Othello* from the Moor's perspective illustrates Bassi's views on the evolving concept of race and its ethical implications. Bassi explores the meaning of being Jewish through the centuries. He emphasizes how the notion of blood is strictly related to the concept of life. Inasmuch as this vital fluid can be contaminated, the survival of the human body, and the ethnic group as a political body at large, is easily at stake. Purification rites are necessary to cure the so-called disease resulting from intermixing (when referred to individuals of different ethnic groups) or invisibility (when referred to an ethnic group that represents a minority within the societal group of a political body) (Bassi, *Essere* 111-12).

In his essay "In the Ghetto," Phillips (53) argues that "the Jew is still Europe's nigger." He quotes James Baldwin – "the Jew must see that he is part of the history of Europe, and will always be so considered by the descendant of the slave" (qtd. in "Ghetto" 52) – to explain his identification with the Jews:

> The bloody excess of colonialism, the pillage and rape of modern Africa, the transportation of 11 million black people to the Americas, and their subsequent bondage were not on the curriculum, and certainly not on the television screen. As a result I vicariously channelled a part of my hurt and frustration through the Jewish experience. ("Ghetto" 54)

As a child at first, and an adult later, Phillips realizes that Europe "still shudders with guilt at mention of the Holocaust" ("Ghetto" 53) and seems to forget its past marked by the stain of colonialism. With Rothberg's (66-107) view in mind that the Holocaust was not unique among human-perpetrated horrors we can trace a parallel between the deportation of African people from their villages to the Americas and the deportation of Jewish people to the death camps, as the omniscient narrator tells us in *The Nature of Blood*:

> After three days of travelling, clamour had finally given way to silence and people were beginning to doze off […] Lying in straw sodden with faeces and vomit, all classes and social distinctions had disappeared. [Eva] watched as a young boy, like the rest of them crazy with

thirst, licked the sweat from his mother's fevered arm. (155-61)

The journey of the enslaved African people is one of the central concerns of Phillips's literature, whether by implication, as in *The Nature of Blood*, or in detail. One example is provided in Phillips's novel, *The Lost Child* (2015), where the narrating voice informs us of the middle passage of the unnamed female character:

> On her journey to the Indies it was the rats that had inspired the greatest fear, for they fed with conviction and grew huge and profited handsomely from their passage. The human cargo was chained and manacled in the hold […] Soon they were too nauseated to eat, and most were too grief-stricken to cry, and she lay surrounded by the doleful mourning of those who rotted in the darkness. (5)

In the two quoted accounts of deportation the similarities in the depiction of inhuman travelling conditions are striking. Despite the passing of time and the impressive scientific/technological developments that have brought about better living conditions for much of humankind, human nature with all its intolerant, destructive urges has remained largely unaltered.

The fourth character, Malka, provides evidence of further similarities between the African and Jewish diasporas:

> *I ask you, is this home? […] Four of us, we live in one cramped apartment. This Holy Land did not deceive us. The people did. The man at the hostel, he said to us, 'Welcome, my black brothers and sisters' […] My people never killed themselves. […] You say you rescued me. Gently plucked me from one century, helped me to cross two more, and then placed me in this time. Here. Now.*

> *But why? What are you trying to prove?* (208; emphasis in the original)

There is a note of sarcasm in Malka's words. The "you" in the last question could refer to history, i.e. the history of white colonial Europe, and the ironic choice of words in "gently plucked me," a verb more commonly associated with fruit or inanimate objects, recalls, once again, the dehumanization and abduction of black Africans during the slave trade.

Frantz Fanon explores the meaning of being black or "not only a nigger" in the Western culture: "You come too late, much too late, there will always be a world – a white world between you and us" (qtd. in Bhabha, *Location* 339). Homi K. Bhabha supports this thought emphasizing that, in modern times, "the figure of the 'human' comes to be *authorized*", but a black human being still is "a member of the marginalized, the displaced, the diasporic." (*Location* 339; emphasis in the original).

On a formal level, the novel's stream of consciousness narrative can be read as an attempt to address this absence of the "Other" from our history. The marginalized condition described by Bhabha and the disconnected fragments both underscore the fact that our history is incomplete (because it has not included the voice of the displaced, of the non-white) and challenge us to cross "borders and boundaries" (*New World* 5) while listening to/engaging with these very human voices whose common denominator is the experience of prejudice based on skin complexion in a Western world divided into two colours: white and non-white. It is a civilized world where the so-called superior human beings often forget the common colour of blood: red.

Phillips covers the concept of "one blood" in his novel *Cambridge* (1991), where the so-called white superior individual conveniently tends to omit the recognition of equality, justice and freedom of the "Other" subjected to white culture and civilization. In the following passage Cambridge quotes a line from the King James Bible:

I, Olumide, who had become black Tom, then David Henderson, and now Cambridge, had broken one of God's commandments. [...] I say again: Pardon the liberty I take in unburdening myself with these hasty lines, but the truth as it is understood by David Henderson (known as Cambridge) is all that I have sought to convey. Praise be the Lord! He who *'hath made of one blood all nations of men for to dwell on all the face of the earth'*. (*Cambridge* 167; quoting Acts 17:26; emphasis mine)

Cambridge's formal register points to the missed potentialities of cross-cultural encounters.[7] The British Empire as colonizer proclaimed itself as the bearer of culture, civilization, and Christian religious beliefs (Fergusson 12). Paradoxically, as Phillips eloquently underscores, Christian religion and proper use of English adopted from the colonizers reinforce the dependence on whiteness in a repetitive pattern of subjugation.

In his comparative and interdisciplinary approach to Holocaust and postcolonial studies, Rothberg (94) links "colonialism to Nazism and racism to anti-Semitism," making visible the connection between the Jewish diaspora and "its relation to blackness." It may be argued that Rothberg's construction of analogies between the Holocaust and colonialism replicates, to a certain degree, Phillips's attempt to induce his readers to engage in a wide, kaleidoscopic investigation of seemingly different past events. The next sections of this study deal with

---

[7] Cambridge's first person narrative borrows from slave narratives such as that of Equiano. Similarly to Equiano's experience, Cambridge's life starts in Africa, continues in England, where he becomes a Christian and a free man, but ends in the West Indies as a slave. Differently from Equiano, Cambridge was accused of the killing of the white overseer Arnold Brown: "the *Christian* Cambridge was conveyed to the capital, where he took his trial for murder. He was found guilty and condemned to suffer death by hanging" (174; emphasis in the original).

both diasporas and how, at certain moments in the novel, they intertwine or parallel each other.

2 The Jewish Question

2.1 Fragmented Narrative

As we saw in the previous chapter, despite the importance of the characters' ethnicities, personal stories and their lived experiences, I am of the opinion that it is history, in its non-linear aspect and constantly recurring variations of certain themes, which proves to be the primary focus of *The Nature of Blood*. Furthermore, Phillips's technique of fragmented storytelling provides an alternative view of the past. My intent in this chapter is to reflect on individual instances of this alternative portrayal in order to explore the novel's comprehensive, more inclusive view of history.

Like Phillips, other intellectuals reject traditional, single-narrative interpretations of history that create the appearance of stability, permanence, and continuity. Michel Foucault, for instance, argues against the so-called evolutionary myth that is often associated with the natural course of events explanation of the past. He raises objections to the unquestioned assumptions that regard history as a cluster of orderly sequenced facts as well as to history as a mere relationship between human beings and the past. Foucault encourages, instead, a study of history that is able to emphasize the multiple cause-and-effect relationships among events (Caruso, "Conversazione" 104-05).

Foucault's interest in establishing connections among past events – not necessarily in chronological sequence or limited to specific locations – offers the opportunity to draw parallels, anticipate circumstances and avert mistakes previously made. In *The Nature of Blood*, Phillips, through the characters of Stephan, Eva, the African General and Malka, apparently attempts to provide evidence of the existence of such links, supporting Foucault's multi-perspective approach to history. The four stories show the similarity between apparently distinct historical events – such as slavery, discrimination, racism – and point to parallels between the experience of African victims of the cross-

Atlantic slave trade and that of European Jews deported to German concentration camps. Phillips's reflections shift from Africa, at the centre of European colonial expansion and of the slave trade, to Europe, where the prejudice against Jews has its origin, magnified across the centuries and culminating in the murderous master race ideology of the German Nazis.

2.1.1 Stephan

Stephan in *The Nature of Blood* may initially appear as a minor character; in truth he represents the core of the whole narration and as such offers a fresh understanding of history. The present study is deeply indebted to Rothberg's work on the Holocaust which also extends to the context of decolonization. He chiefly deals with the concept of "memory as *multidirectional*" (3; emphasis in the original). History and memory turn out to be dependent on each other, which makes it possible to investigate past events with a multidirectional vision.

My purpose is to draw connections between the gaps in the novel's stories in order to reveal recurring patterns between seemingly isolated events in history. Stephan's narrative operates as a frame, while his character functions as a hub. The frame contains the fragmented stories; the hub can be viewed as the focal point through which they pass. If we accept Foucault's suggestion in regard to the understanding of history, the hub, Stephan, becomes a point of convergence from where multiple connections among historical events radiate.

Only on rare occasions does Stephan recount his story directly. We get the opportunity to know him through the voices of Eva and the omniscient narrator, who fills in the gaps in the narrative left by the first person narrating voices. Stephan is the first character we are introduced to, but his identity emerges only from his niece's reminiscences of her adolescence:

> And then we saw the photographs of Uncle Stephan. He was tall and strong, and he stared confidently into the camera with his soft eyes. Seeing him again sent my mind spinning back six years to when he visited the house. I was about to speak, when I felt the outside of Margot's shoe scuff my ankle, and I knew that I should not comment upon these photographs. Five of them spread across two pages. Uncle Stephan. Always on his own. Always staring directly into the lens of the camera. Always standing.
> Uncle Stephan was Papa's only brother. He had journeyed to the British colony of Palestine, for he wanted to defend the new Jewish settlements against attacks from the Arabs, and to prepare the land for large-scale settlement by Jews of all ages and backgrounds. However, his journey was made all the more arduous by the fact that in order to visit this so-called promised land he had to leave behind a young wife and child, and break off from his medical studies. (72)

Eva depicts her uncle in a few concise phrases. Stephan's aplomb is stressed by the adverb 'always' along with the way he poses in front of the camera; whereas the repetition of 'stare,' 'camera' and 'always' confers a sort of rhythm to Eva's words. Eva introduces the relative who is regarded as a failure, if not as a disgrace, by his family. He is just a memory confined to the past whose existence is proved by photographs that are kept in "the old photograph album" (71). When Eva's mother has to decide which family belonging to bring to the small apartment "instead of stuffing it into a suitcase or a bag, or leaving it on the huge pile of materials whose fate was yet to be decided, she set it down on the drawing-room table and dusted its cover with a cloth" (71). The description of "Mama" wiping the photo album reinforces the Sterns' ambivalent feelings towards their family member.

The images of Stephan are not exhibited where guests are entertained. In truth, Stephan is unknown to his niece, too:

> I remember the day when I returned home from school and saw the fancy leather valise in the hallway. […] We had a visitor. In the drawing room sat a tall sun-tanned man, delicately holding a cup of coffee between his broad hands. Papa sat opposite him, the two men engaged in an animated conversation. When I walked in, Papa looked up and Uncle Stephan turned to face me.
> 'Ah, and here she is. Little Eva. Eva, do you remember my brother, Stephan?'
> Of course, I didn't. I smiled nervously. (73)

We gradually understand the reason for these controversial feelings. Eva's first memory of her uncle is the one of "a visitor […] engaged in an animated conversation" with her father. In addition, during his staying at Eva's house, "In the evenings, Papa and Uncle Stephan would sit together, their conversation growing louder and more heated as the evening wore on" (75). The two brothers seem unable to talk without turning the conversation into an intense dispute that ultimately leads to distinct differences:

> After a week of acrimony and raised voices, Uncle Stephan crossed a bridge and passed into the world of himself. […] Uncle Stephan returned to Palestine, he disappeared without trace. […] Only now […] I realize how desperately unhappy Papa must have been. Papa needed his family. He needed his wife. He needed his daughters. He needed his brother. […] Mama looked on helplessly, and then she smiled in the directions of the girls. (76-80)

As we perceive from Eva's last reminiscences of her uncle, we sense why the photograph album was "out of [...] reach" (71).

Stephan's brother and wife do not comprehend or approve of his dedication to the cause of the promised land. This emerges from his niece's reluctance to comment on the photographs. The reason for this disapproval lies, once again, in Eva's memories:

> Papa was adamant. Uncle Stephan had given up on his medical studies, discarded a wife and daughter, and gone off to fight for what? Why create another home among these Arab people? His wife was right to refuse to uproot her life and expose her child to these barbarians. Papa and he could set up in medical practice together. The brothers Stern. They might become the richest doctors in the country. Why had Stephan suddenly become a fool who evaded his responsibilities? [...] Uncle did not like being a called a fool, and this epithet generally produced a vocal storm which raged and bellowed as long as the pair of them had the energy. Had Ernst forgotten that they were Jews? That they remained the only people on the face of the earth without their own home. Did he know this? (75)

The two brothers embrace different purposes, but they have in common the trait of resoluteness. Papa/Ernst represents a typical family man: he is settled down, married, father of two daughters and practices a respectable profession. The reality of the world outside his house does not seem to be a main concern for him. Conversely, Stephan dedicates his life to the *"House of Israel"* (201; emphasis in the original) and for his cause, he is ready "to leave behind a young wife and child" (73) and accept being "always on his own" (72). Stephan does not hide the sacrifice required by his quest to reclaim "our troubled land. Palestine. Israel" (3). Since the beginning of the novel – on the island of Cyprus of all places where Jewish refugees find a shelter before heading to the promised land – Stephan informs us of his marital status: "'Do you have a wife?' 'No,' I said. 'At least, not any more. She is in America with my daughter'" (8). Nonetheless, he mentions them on a regular basis, and sometimes without hiding his regret:

> Enough killing. Now there will be a homeland. Yes. We can share. And so to finish my medical studies. And for some time now, simply a doctor. I never tried to find my wife and child. She wrote to me, saying that she respected my choice and she asked me to respect hers. She never wished to see me again. And now it is too late. I have let them go. Let them go. (11)

Stephan never uses their names, an indication that he has managed to "let them go." Respectful of Stephan's great personal sacrifice, the omniscient narrator briefly introduces Renate, a woman whom Stephan had fallen in love with, but still refers to the mother of Stephan's daughter as "his wife" (204):

> Over the years there had, of course, been entanglements, including one protracted relationship with a musician, a cellist from Austria, whose daughter he had treated for bronchitis. Now, as he looked back almost thirty years, he had come to recognize this as probably the love of his life. Not including, of course, his wife. Since Renate, the cellist, there had been occasional and generally unsatisfactory encounters. (203-04)

At certain points in the novel, the omniscient narrator provides personal details about Stephan's life in Israel:

Ten years ago, after his retirement, he had decided to sell his city-centre apartment, for he imagined that the profit would ease his remaining years. His new apartment [...] was comfortable although somewhat noisy. [...] A little over two years ago, he had nearly died. It was after his recuperation that he decided to join the club, for, with neither work nor family to occupy him, he had finally admitted to himself that he was lonely. (200)

We understand that Stephan has achieved much of what he had hoped to achieve when he left Europe, and he has earned some level of material comfort, but the condition of solitude, already alluded to by Eva, still persists. He is aware of the consequences of having chosen one path – one that matched his ideals – rather than the one proposed by his brother, who seemed unaffected by the rise of the Nazi party, at least until the moment he and his family had to face the reality of the concentration camps.

Loneliness is the price that Stephan has to pay for his quest. However, Stephan "understood that people are not made to live alone, neither when things are good, nor when they are bad" (211) and becomes a member of a local club:

The management's chief source of income were the men, who were required to pay an annual membership fee for their weekly flights of fantasy. Other activities were continually promised, such as outings to places of historical interest, informal dinners, and lectures by prominent speakers on issues relating to the culture and arts of the country. However, in the two years that he had been a member, he was not aware of any other club activities, beyond these weekly dances each Wednesday afternoon. (199-200)

Though the programme is appealing, the real intent is to provide lonely men with "weekly flights of fantasy." The promise of arts and culture lends a surface appearance of high-minded respectability to a club which, as the narrator clearly reveals, merely exploits the members' longing for company for a fee:

> Some of the men travelled in from nearby kibbutzim, but the majority lived in the city. They were elderly, mainly bachelors or widowers, but among them were those whose loveless marriages had long ago turned stale. A few among the young women were prostitutes, but the greater number of them were students, or unemployed actresses, all of whom were paid a small sum by the management to dance for a few hours each week. (199)

Stephan is struck by Malka: "He had been watching her for a long time. [...] this woman was beautiful. He could not take his eyes from her" (198). They spend the night together in a hotel room because "To his neighbours, he was a respectable retired bachelor doctor" (204). The same apprehensiveness of being seen with a young African woman from the club and judged emerges, once again, the morning after when he walks along the promenade to enjoy "a clear view of the sea" (211):

> What are you doing in town? So early? I saw you last night. With a black woman. No, it was you. I am sure of it. He saw a bench which nobody had yet claimed [...] He sat heavily and tried not to think of his wife and child. But it was useless. Every day, assaulted by loneliness. Every day, eaten up with guilt. His only companion was memory. (211)

In the above passage, the omniscient narrator depicts a weary Stephan suffering from the burden of loneliness and guilt. His regret about abandoning a loving family for his ambitious project haunts him. The last phrase recalls the metaphor of the hub proposed above. Daniel L. Schacter defines the act of remembering as "a telescope pointed at time" (*Searching for Memory* 15). Cognitive scientists compare the human brain to a computer in which information is stored; when our subjective past experiences are retrieved, we are released from restriction of time and place (Schacter 16-17). When this telescope of memory leads us to re-experience past events, then a remembered time and location overlap with the present time and location. This can be applied to the reading of the novel and its unconventional recounting of history. The narrated episodes may then be regarded as subjective experiences. Stephan/the hub may be compared to a human brain where the episodes or subjective experiences are stored, while in my view the act of reading becomes a training for the historical memory that releases us from the restrictions of time and place. Ultimately, this can also be regarded as an alternative metaphor for Phillips's passion for literature, a passion that allows him to transgress boundaries, and such travel can be achieved by exercizing the historical memory. This time travel of sorts occurs in the novel when the mental image of the ageing Stephan who sits on the bench to enjoy "a clear view of the [Israeli] sea" (211) echoes the mental image that takes shape in our minds in accordance with how the omniscient narrator ends the novel: "alone on the bench, his arms outstretched, reaching across the years" (212).

Both moments on the bench are devoted to reflections that lead to remembering, and in those instants different time and location overlap the actual ones as perceived in the phrases "tried not to think of his wife and child. But it was useless" (211) and "his arms outstretched, reaching across the years." However, two opposite intentions mark those moments: in Israel, a mature Stephan is led to remember by his guilt and embarks on a journey back to his past life; whereas in Germany a young Stephan is open to embark on a journey into the future.

The character of Stephan raises the issue of prejudice. Phillips seems to point out that nobody is impartial and capable of objective consideration. This emerges from the following passage:

> In the morning, she was gone. His first thought was to make sure that his wallet was still in his jacket pocket, but he resisted this ungenerous impulse. [...] she belonged to another land. She might be happier there. Dragging these people from their primitive world into this one, and in such a fashion, was not a policy with which he had agreed. They belonged to another place. (210)

Stephan's bigotry may appear as a little perplexing for most readers, given the character's past, particularly his involvement in the struggle to establish a promised land. We would expect him to be sympathetic and understanding towards "these people," fellow Jews, who, like himself, are recent arrivals in Israel. His disapproval of their transplantation "from their primitive world" (cf. 2.1.3) echoes Ernst's displeasure with Stephan's commitment to Zionism. Both men go so far as to employ the same word, 'primitive,' to refer to what they perceive to be non-white/non-European lands:

> *(Why create another home? We can set up in practice together. The brothers Stern. We might become the richest doctors in the country.)* [...] *(To this primitive British colony of Palestine? I have dutifully bought the stamps to pay for the land that you buy from the Arabs. I have done my duty. Enough of this foolishness.)* (10; emphasis in the original)

As Jews, Stephan and Ernst are representatives of the best-known and best-documented diaspora in human history, but when Ernst labels the "Other" (in this case the Arabs) as "*primitive*," he is adopting the malevolent attitude of the colonizer. Here Phillips implies that while temporal, geographical and political contexts may vary, the presence of racially and culturally based prejudice is a stubbornly recurring phenomenon throughout history. Ledent (*Caryl Phillips* 140) offers one explanation for the persistence of bigotry: "however reassuring for the individual, a feeling of attachment may prove destructive in the long term, as it tends to petrify biases and turn former victims of racism into racists." The ageing Stephan experiences precisely this kind of attachment: his attachment to the land of Israel, which he had idealized and helped build prevents him from accommodating the evolving multicultural reality of modern Israel. Similarly, Ernst, though aware he is not entirely accepted as a German, has managed to develop a feeling of attachment that allows him to consider Germany "*home*."

It has to remain open whether the name of Stern used in the novel is meant to allude to the "Stern Gang." [1]

---

[1] In August 1940, in Mandatory Palestine, Avraham Stern founded Lehi, (an acronym from *Lohamei Herust Israel* – Fighters for the Freedom of Israel) also known as the Stern Gang, with the intent of evicting the British authorities from Palestine and reversing the restrictive immigration quotas of Jews to Palestine imposed by London. They also hoped to establish a totalitarian Hebrew republic in the territory. The Stern Gang was so adverse to British authorities that it organized and launched terrorist attacks against the British (Hart 267-68). As an activist, Avraham Stern was so single-mindedly obsessed with achieving the narrow goals of his organization that during the Second World War he even attempted to form an alliance with the Nazis. He believed that "the enemy of my enemy is my friend" and hoped that with German assistance, he could overthrow British rule and make it possible for all European Jews to return to Israel (Hart 270-71). Stern's controversial views isolated him politically and militarily. In 1942 he was killed by British CID (Criminal Investigation Department) (Shindler 218).

Caryl Phillips replied to my query regarding this matter thus: "I suspect that 'Stern' is more related to the rather straight-forward fact that my history teacher at school was called Ernest Sterne – he was a German Jewish refugee from Berlin who arrived in Leeds in the late thirties. Strange how the imagination works" (private email, 6 Oct 2017).

Despite the extremism of groups like Stern's Lehi, Zionism has been primarily a political Jewish nationalist movement. However, the radical fringe of the movement, embodied by Avraham Stern's totalitarian and racist ideology, never entirely ceased to exist (Siragusa, prefazione 5-18).

Stephan's devotion to the cause of the promised land comprises some of the aims and contradictions of the Stern Gang as well as aspects of political Zionism. Despite its religious, non-belligerent orientation (at its heart, it is a movement that aspires to create a state based on Jewish religious values), Zionism's all-volunteer army also conducted military operations. Referring to the paramilitary *Hagannah* in Palestine, Stephan says: "'I, too, was in the army before I became a doctor. But, Moshe, the army is not everything. *Hagannah* is not everything. A wife and child, now that is something'" (8; emphasis in the original). Stephan is aware of the personal trade-off that such absolute devotion to a cause entails, namely the absence of family life and loneliness. That is not to say that he questions his decision: "Yes, the army [...] will make sure that you continue to have a home" (7-11).

Stephan's idealistic vision of a homeland for all Jews becomes tainted by his racist feelings towards other Jews who do not rise to what he expects a Jew to be, as we saw earlier in relation to his views on Ethiopian immigrants (cf. 2.1.3). Transferring Ethiopian Jews to Israel is part of the reason for founding a Jewish homeland. But in the case of Stephan, a white, European-born and educated doctor, the old continent's sense of cultural and racial superiority gets the better of political idealism and empathy towards darker-skinned Jews.

Stephan's lack of empathy towards African Jews escaping hardship might be hard to understand given his own Jewish experience, but the sentiment is hardly unusual throughout history. In 1946 "the British had initiated their policy of turning away refugee ships from Palestine, and off-loading the passengers on to their island of Cyprus" (5). Stephan informs us of "the British quota of seven hundred and fifty persons per month [, which] meant that thousands would have to spend weeks, if not years, under British lock and key on Cyprus" (5). Paradoxically, the survivors of the atrocities of the war had to shamefully wait in internment camps "containing over thirty thousand refugees of all ages and nationalities, whose sole aim in life was to escape war-ravaged Europe and reach the promised land" (5). It was during this forced stopover, in an attempt to ease the refugees' psychological distress, that

> Mr Bellow had been sent to Cyprus by a New York-based Jewish aid organization, the Joint Distribution Committee. [...] The benevolent Mr Bellow, a large, jocular man, presided over all the camps, attending to the health, education and general welfare of the displaced and the dispossessed. He faithfully promised each internee that they would eventually reach Palestine. [...] It was Mr Bellow who had arranged for trained professionals to journey from Palestine, both to attend to the sick and to assist in social welfare and language training. Quite simply, we professionals were to prepare these internees for their future lives. (5)

Stephan premises that among "we professionals" there are also "armed emissaries from Palestine who regularly infiltrate [...] the camp" (5). These emissaries are "*Hagannah* trainees, secretly preparing themselves for a life of military service in the underground army that they would join once they reached Palestine" (5).

Stephan's words come at the very beginning of the novel and introduce the theme of exile and diaspora. Beth Rosenberg (39-40) points out the importance of geographical spaces and boundaries when "the origin of national identity" becomes a concern for those people who are considered "illegal aliens" and whose return to their homeland is denied. For the Jewish refugees on Cyprus the effects produced by such circumstance create a division between the extremists who aim to forcefully repossess Palestine and expel the British and the Arabs, on the one hand , and "the innocents," in Mr Bellow's words, those "in need of constant protection and education" on the other (5). Moshe, one of the latter, asks about a place whose real meaning is unknown to him. As an attempt to soothe his worries and uncertainties, Stephan portrays the promised land as an idyllic, paradisiac place, a sort of Garden of Eden:

> 'And in Israel the fruit is on the trees?'
> 'The fruit is on the trees. You may take the fruit straight from the branch.'
> [...]
> 'Do you think I will find a wife?'
> I laughed now.
> 'Moshe, you will be able to choose from hundreds of pretty women.'
> [...]
> 'You will marry a beautiful girl and have wonderful children. And, sure, you will join the army if you wish.'
> (3-9)

Stephan merely provides a generic image of a home rather than an authentic depiction of an actual place. In truth, it is hard to define home in an objective, precise way as each human being attaches their own personal experiences, values and memories to the word: home can be a physical space, feeling, practices, and/or an active state of being in the world. In relation to the concept of home, Phillips ("Necessary Journeys" 124) reminds us of the significance of time and boundaries: "I not only belong to the British tradition, but I am also a writer of African origin, and for African diasporan people, 'home' is a word that is often burdened with a complicated historical and geographical weight."

The idyllic image employed by Stephan to describe the promised land allows me to draw a brief parallel with the African diaspora that dates back to the Atlantic slave trade between the sixteenth and the nineteenth centuries. According to Stephen Howe (13), in the imagination of African victims of the transatlantic slave trade and their descendants, Africa is an idealized motherland, it "is an imaginary place, [...] a mythography of conquering kings, superheroes, and bucolic bliss." Howe's words could equally be applied to Stephan's depiction of Palestine.

In addition to the special resonance of diaspora and the idealized vision of home and return for them, African and Jewish ethnic groups have in common the dream of a unifying project. The twofold ends of such a project are the provision of a home for dispersed peoples and, as a desirable side effect, the creation of a common cause for people to rally around and feel as one. Africa and Palestine, respectively, are the goals of Pan-Africanism and Zionism.

Originally, the notion of Pan-Africanism refers to the unity of all continental Africa and is grounded on the idea that peoples of African descent have common interests and should be unified. However, over time the concept of Pan Africanism absorbed other meanings as well. These are summarized by Howe (25) as follows:

1. The aspiration for political co-operation, and awareness of a common experience of discrimination, among peoples of African descent (wherever they may live) [...]
2. The claim that people of African descent, wherever they live, have and should rediscover common sociocultural traditions derived from their shared origins. Some versions of this belief speak in terms of a distinctive 'African personality' involving shared philosophies, attitude to life, or modes of expression and behaviour. In the Francophone world this latter variant came to be known as *négritude* [...] More recently in the Anglophone

world, and especially the USA, similar beliefs have adopted the title Afrocentrism.
3. Belief in the need for the political unity, or at least much closer political, economic and cultural co-operation, between the states of the African continent. [...]
4. [...] in South Africa, Pan Africanism has become the political label of those who tend to stress the racial element in group conflict and identity as against emphasis on social class, political ideology or universalist principles.

Pan-Africanist ideas first began to circulate in the mid-nineteenth century in the United States within the American colonization movement. In the early twentieth century, W.E.B. Du Bois gave the movement a political slant and asserted that the problem of the twentieth century is the issue of the colour line, which is not confined merely to the United States and its "Negro Problem." In the wake of World War II, Pan Africanism developed into an openly anti-imperial movement (Howe 25-26). However, the movement is not immune from criticism in regard to its integrity. Kehinde Andrews, for instance, points to some existing connections between Pan-Africanist leaders and the former British Empire. In particular, Andrews underlines the issue of education and reminds us that "colonialism could only be carried out with the help of a native bourgeois class who would impart Western wisdom in the colonies." Furthermore, "the civil servants and future leaders of Africa and the Caribbean were trained and educated in the West, with Britain being a key landing point." This means that they were and are deeply influenced by a culture that was (a) imposed on them for the purpose of turning them into instruments of colonial control and (b) which does not recognize them as equal participants in the culture (Andrews 2508-11).

In *The Atlantic Sound*, Phillips recounts his personal triangular trade journey. He visits Liverpool (UK), Elmina (Ghana) and Charleston (USA). In Elmina, Phillips attends Panafest – "'the biggest gathering of the African family to celebrate our cultural unity. Artists and intellectuals of Africa and the diaspora are gathering together as a family in Mother Africa, in order that they might celebrate their values'" (114). However, he cannot help noticing how the movement is far from the unity aspired to by the organizers, in part because of "the intrusion of Europe" (115) that is still pervasive, but also because of differences among black communities that are scattered throughout the world.

The encounter with an African citizen on the plane to Elmina makes Phillips aware of his enduring fragmented nature, or "my plural self" ("Necessary Journeys" 123) due to having Caribbean parents, his African ancestors and his skin complexion because "as a boy growing up in England, I knew that the main factor preventing my full participation in British life was the color of my skin" ("Color" 11):

> In our short time together I have listened to him sing a discordant anthem of indignation. Like me, he is, in part, the product of British imperial adventures. Unlike me, he is an African. A Ghanaian. A whole man. A man of one place. A man who will never flinch at *the* question, 'Where are you from?' A man going home. [...] Ben is returning home. [...] I envy his rootedness. (*Atlantic Sound* 100; emphasis in the original)

Like Zionism, Pan-Africanism is divided into separate branches. In 2007, Achille Mbembe defined Afropolitanism as "something beyond Pan-Africanism":

> Afropolitanism refers to a way – the many ways – in which Africans, or people of African origin, understand themselves as being part of the world rather than being apart. Historically, Africa has been defined in the Hege-

lian paradigm as out of history, as not belonging to the world – as being some region of the planet which has no significance whatsoever in terms of the real history of the human in the world. But of course, that is not true. Afropolitanism is a name for undertaking a critical reflection on the many ways in which, in fact, there is no world without Africa and there is no Africa that is not part of it. So that's the philosophical inflection of the term. (Mbembe and Balakrishnan 29)

Mbembe views Pan Africanism as largely "a racial ideology." Unlike African Americans who consider Africa as the source of their culture, the point of origin of their intellectual views as well as their art, Afropolitanism has a global vision that is not based on the location of the African continent. Mbembe highlights the crucial role played by the continent in Western history, especially starting from the fifteenth century and the beginning of the slave trade. Western economies, in particular, have relied and still rely on Africa. In the current context of displacement and south-north migration, the issue of the dispossessed African people becomes "a planetary reading of our predicament [because] Afrocentrism is a geography of circulation and mobility" (Mbembe and Balakrishnan 30-34).

2.1.2 Eva

2.1.2.1 Cyprus

The Nature of Blood devotes more pages to Eva then to any other character. Eva's narrative combined with the information provided by the omniscient narrator, makes up the largest portion of the novel.

Before introducing herself, Eva provides some general details about her life along with self-effacing remarks mixed with a need to reassure (or possibly preserve her distance from) others, such as "I will be fine. There is nothing to worry about. I have survived this long" (13), or "Do not come any closer. My breath is foul with disease and tooth decay" (25), as well as "I will be new and I will look graceful" (31). These details depict an afflicted human being; however, they bewilder readers; it is not easily perceived whom this stream of consciousness is addressing. As narrator, Eva gives an account of her family, which seems more of an attempt to re-establish her point of origin than an introduction of her parents and sister:

> My Mama has left me alone [...] Her husband was a well-respected man, a young doctor, who eventually provided her with a beautiful four-storey house and two daughters. [...] Mama's sense of herself became the source of much of Papa's unhappiness, but Margot and I did not understand this until it was too late. [...] I roll on to my side and steer my thoughts towards Margot. She is all I have left. If I can find Margot, then perhaps together we might rebuild a life. (13-17)

The "too late" in relation to her parents contrasts with the "might" in the last sentence, which conveys Eva's aspiration to reunite with her sister and make a fresh start. The slow rhythm that characterizes the recounting of her experiences and feelings emphasizes her condition as a deeply traumatized survivor of extreme violence. Eva's emotional burden, which will be elaborated on in the following pages, emerges from her stream of consciousness.

It is as if Eva alleviates her pain through a dialogue with the reader. Among the various treatments Freud proposed for mental disorders, the autobiographical process is especially relevant for the purpose of discussing Eva's story. Freud identified autobiography as an alternative method for catharsis that, in his own words, aims "to construct a narrative in which subjective and objective attitudes, biographical and historical interests are combined in a new proportion" (Freud, *Autobiographical Study* 7). This process of self-analysis may be regarded as clinical practice. The self-analysis is to help the individual to talk about a trauma which renders the recounting of what happened unspeakable. This clinical practice does not necessarily require the psychoanalyst's presence. A healing of emotional blockages can also be achieved through uninhibited talking, and the private self-dialogue is conducive to a freer flow of words, memories and ideas. Current theorists still support this practice; Judith Lewis Herman (1), for instance, asserts that "the conflict between the will to deny horrible events and the will to proclaim them aloud is the central dialectic of psychological trauma." Trauma triggers feelings of shame and fear, as a result of which survivors of tragedy are often deprived of their voice. When secrecy prevails, the story of the traumatic event appears, not as verbal narrative, but as symptom or re-enactment. The attempt of telling one's story potentially enables the individual to regain a sense of continuity and wholeness (Richman 639).

In *The Nature of Blood*, readers find themselves before a similar type of autobiographical process. Eva reveals both internal and external experiences in an uncensored form without adhering to a meticulous plan. Sometimes her reminiscences are interwoven with immediate experiences; at other times, they will unexpectedly shift in time and place. Phillips's writing style itself draws attention to and helps guide the reader through this autobiographical process. Eva's reflections are fragmented, but fragments are distinctly demarcated by a blank space to indicate a pause. Elsewhere, fragments are characterized by the repetition of key words which give the passage a compulsive, circular quality as in a passage shortly after Eva has left the concentration camp:

> I sit outside the hut and stare at the sky. Tonight, I will not sleep. My head is full of worries. I worry about Papa. I worry about Mama. I worry about Margot. I worry about what else I might have done. Between torn patches of cloud, the sky is choked with stars. This night air is warm and clammy. I worry because there is nobody to help guide me in the right direction. I have never been alone. There has always been somebody. And now there seems to be just me and the night and the sky. (24)

The noun 'worry' is repeated seven times in total, but it is the word 'sky' in the first and last sentences that frames Eva's list of worries about what may have happened to her family, her solitude and her guilt. Another instance of this kind of framing:

> I spend the afternoon sitting by myself. I have claimed a new berth, out in the open, in the full glare of the sun, close to the fence. I sit on a pile of discarded timber, squeezing myself into a crevice which holds me as though it were a comfortable chair. From this position, I can watch the sunlight moving like a cat along the palings of the fence. Since Mama left, I have grown accustomed to being solitary. But these days, even if I wished for company I would probably find myself alone. Tears begin to well in my eyes. These past years have hurt me in mind and body. I sit on this pile of wood. Close to the fence. On a warm spring afternoon. (29)

This time it is the word 'afternoon' that frames the beginning and end of a series of thoughts revolving around separation from others. Eva constantly makes mental notes of her personal experiences and feelings, perhaps in an effort to recognize patterns and thus gain some control over her overwhelming feelings of pain, solitude and dehumanization. Despite her liberation from the camp, she does not yet see herself as fully human, comparing herself to a cat, still unsure of her freedom – she is "out in the open" but "close to the fence" –, in a condition of mental, if not physical, captivity. However, the circular arrangement of these reflections seems to indicate an attempt to regain a sense of wholeness.

In Eva's autobiographical process, we also perceive her effort to re-establish a daily routine, and she seems to find encouragement watching birds in flight:

> I like the way birds fly. At first you see the effort, how they flap their wings frantically as they build up speed and direction. And then they stop and glide confidently. And then comes my favourite part, when they suddenly start to flap their wings again and build up speed. That's what I do these days. I just sit here on my timber and watch the birds beyond the fence. I watch their communal flight. Every day, they beat a thin black ribbon across the sky. There are too many to give them names, or to get to know them personally. I just sit here on my timber and watch them. Every day. My name is Eva Stern. I am twenty-one years old. Just when I think I am going to fall, I flap my wings. (35)

Although Eva is still using non-human imagery to describe herself, there is now a hopeful confidence in the metaphor of a bird flapping its wings to control its course. The passive, powerless young woman who sees herself as an immobile, watchful cat lying among the "discarded timber" (29) of a few pages earlier is slowly re-discovering her agency and looking for ways to survive the aftermath of war and the traumatic experience of the concentration camp.

In the succession of narrating voices, Eva's enters the narrative flow in the first pages, giving evidence of her traumatized condition:

> I WATCH as the trucks come roaring into the camp, dust and mud flying up behind their wheels. As the men jump down to the ground, they whistle and shout to each other. Then silence descends over them. They shield their eyes and look about themselves in disbelief. Silence. I count fifteen vehicles. The men are standing and staring at us. These men who are bursting with health. Some put their hands to their mouths and noses, while others pull handkerchiefs from their pockets and jam them into their faces. It is hard to know what they are thinking, but, whatever it is, they are struggling. This silent scene of us facing them. Skeletons facing men. Former prisoners facing liberators. We will no longer have to endure this captivity. We are free. These English men have arrived on this warm spring day and now we are free. [...] I have no strength to be happy. My thin bones would shake and fall apart were they to be subjected to such an emotion. (12-13)

Phillips's juxtaposition of sharply contrasting images, expressed in short, sparse sentences, underscores the paradoxes of Eva's liberation: the whistles and shouts turn into silence; men bursting with health are paralysed; skeletons face men; freedom is not accompanied by expressions of happiness. The accumulation of contradictory ideas makes it difficult for us to form a rational response to the scene, leaving us instead to share the characters' feelings of horror and confusion. Liberation is not the end of suffering; the end of the camps is not the return to normality. This joyless, unsettling depiction of a moment that should be happy reaches its apex in the final sentences, when Eva seems to compare herself to an empty, damaged vessel that has been deprived of its organic structure and is no longer capable of experiencing human emotion.

We find Eva in one of the camps set up by Jewish organizations to house survivors:

> Mr Bellow had been sent to Cyprus by a New York-based Jewish aid organization, the Joint Distribution Committee. He had arrived in the Mediterranean shortly after the British had initiated their policy of turning away refugee ships from Palestine, and off-loading the passengers on to their island of Cyprus. At first there were two camps, then three, then four, and now there were almost a dozen, containing over thirty thousand refugees of all ages and nationalities, whose sole aim in life was to escape war-ravaged Europe and reach the promised land. (5)

The above passage is a clear manifestation of the paradoxical circumstances that affected the Jewish diaspora and echoes Arendt's reflections on "contemporary history [that] has created a new kind of human beings – the kind that are put in concentration camps by their foes and in internment camps by their friends" (Arendt, "We refugees" 111).

The voice of the activist Stephan (cf. 2.1.1) informs readers about British policies in regard to the settlement of Jews in Palestine, and, to some degree, the imparting of such detail appears as an attempt to justify the existence of new/shifting forms of confinement: "the British quota of seven hundred and fifty persons per month meant that thousands would have to spend weeks, if not years, under British lock and key on Cyprus" (5). Stephan's concern that Cyprus is yet another prison camp is soon corroborated:

> Up on the hill, and crouched behind the barbed-wire fence, the camp stared down at us. A dishevelled collection of tin huts and tents were illuminated by bright floodlights. However, this shower of electricity, far from conferring any glamour, served only to confirm the pitiful nature of the whole shabby enterprise. The British had taken it upon themselves to imprison the defenceless. (6)

The brutal reality of the Nazis death camp is, in many ways, replicated by the British rescuers, who enclose the Jewish camp survivors on all sides with a "shower of electricity" so as to discourage escapes and outside communication. Moreover, the barbed wire and the floodlight echo the depiction of Bergen-Belsen in the novel: "A forest of barbed-wire illuminated by powerful lights" (171).

Agamben, influenced by Arendt's and Foucault's studies of totalitarianism and biopolitics, develops his own reflections on camps:

> The camp is merely the place in which the most absolute *conditio inhumana* that has ever existed on earth was realized: this is what counts in the last analysis, for the victims as for those who come after. […] Instead of deducing the definition of the camp from the events that took place there, we will ask: What is a camp, what is its juridicopolitical structure that such events could take place there? This will lead us to regard the camp not as historical fact and an anomaly belonging to the past (even if still verifiable) but in some way as the hidden matrix and *nomos* of the political space in which we are still living. (166)

Using as his starting point the concept of *nomos*, i.e. the view that laws are socially constructed and consensual, Agamben (167) asserts that "the camps constitute a space of exception and martial law." Originally, camps were conceived as *Schutzhaft*, whose literally meaning is "protective custody," a police measure to prevent violence directed against organized political communities. Marginalized individuals or *personae non gratae*, may they be criminals or refugees, were confined to a camp outside "the normal juridical order." Expanding on the concept of *Schutzhaft*, Nazi representatives of law and order took "into custody" any individual potentially threatening "the security of the state." However, Agamben reminds us that

> the first concentration camps in Germany were the work not of the Nazi regime but of the Social Democratic governments, which interned thousands of communist militants in 1923 on the basis of *Schutzhaft* and also created the *Konzentrationslager für Ausländer* at Cottbus-Sielow, which housed mainly Eastern European refugees and which may, therefore, be considered the first camp for Jews in this century (even if it was, obviously, not an extermination camp). (167)

Given the origin of the twentieth century German concentration camp, it may be inferred that this practice of inclusion and exclusion based on political beliefs as well as racial prejudice – that is to say eligibility for citizenship or recognition as a "proper" member of the German societal group – is rooted in the German (and arguably many authoritarian societies') cultural DNA.

The atrocities of the Nazi concentration camps affected survivors not only physically. The psychological wounds run deeper and take much longer to heal. In Cyprus, despite her experience of forced confinement during the Nazi years, Eva seems to be more comfortable inside a space surrounded by twisted strands of fence wire than venturing outside:

> I walk close to the barbed-wire fence and peer at the world beyond the camp. I touch the fence. I know where I am. I am suddenly appalled to realize that I am comfortable being confined. To remove the wire seems unthinkable. I know that I am free to trespass on the other side, to saunter out through the gate and bolt in any direction I choose. But looking at life through this fence suits me better. (22)

Based on the metaphor of the bird quoted earlier, Eva may be likened to one of those animals born in captivity and unable to act like its wild peers that avoid enclosed spaces: "Beyond the fence, a bird sets forth from a tree and soars into the air. But even while lost in flight, the bird remains beyond the fence. The bird never flies close to the fence" (22).

Then, Eva provides an unflattering description of life in the confusing purgatory of the Cypriot camp. The occupants of the camp are disoriented and lost in an environment that replicates the death camp but without the clear roles and expectations imposed by the Nazi prison guards:

> Four months in this place. Before this place, I worked. I struggled to keep death at bay. There were small ways of trying to stay alive. Cunning was a skill worth acquiring. As was endurance. Community formed the basis of our lives, but then came the long march, and yet another train, and then this place, which offered no community, no planning, no hope for survival. No work. Merely death. And waiting. I have spent most of the past four months on my cot trying to sleep. No work. And here,

without community, without routine, only the strongest can survive. Every day I have stared death in the face. To become weak is to disappear. And eventually I felt myself becoming indifferent. Nothing bothered me any more. Those of us who have lasted until the arrival of these Englishmen, we have forgotten how to think of tomorrow. (17)

Once again, the political authorities show disregard for Jews as human beings, or to use Arendt's words, first "their [Nazi] foes" and later "their [English] friends" caused feelings of alienation through their dehumanizing treatment. Eva's apathy can be examined using Agamben's study of the inclusion-exclusion relationship that inevitably arises in concentration camps. Individuals, in this case Jews who were excluded by Nazi-German society, try to give a purpose to their disrupted lives, even though it is a distorted gesture in a cruel survival competition – with cunning as a "skill worth acquiring" – rather than a healthy attempt at societal cohesion. The German imprisonment and execution complexes were designed to reduce internees to a subhuman level before their extinction.

In contrast to the "communal flight" of the birds observed by Eva, she has lost her ability to experience community with others during her internment. She deliberately avoids any form of social interaction: "I do not wish to see anything or anybody" (18). She secludes herself from the rest of the society in the camp, and silence seems to be her only wish. When, for example, Gerry, an English soldier, tries to engage her in a conversation, her replies are invariably terse and minimal. Eva is more explicit in the autobiographical process that she shares with the reader; she comments: "I have no desire to pursue this conversation with Gerry […] why is this man talking to me as though we are friends?" (24).

Eva's refusal to talk was not uncommon among former prisoners of the death camps. Silence as a sort of shelter from the feeling of powerlessness among survivors of the Holocaust has been documented in writings released after the end of World War II. One recent example is found in Marcello Kalowski's biography of his father, a survivor of Auschwitz. In the prologue Kalowski writes:

> [I]n Auschwitz some left the camp alive, but no one really survived. These pages pay homage to my father and to those like him – the majority – who witnessed, in silence, the impossibility of tearing down a wall that was erected at a certain point in his life, irrevocably separating that life from the existence that followed.[2] (viii; translation mine)

Kalowski calls attention to the inability to cope with the devastating experience of an internee in a death camp. The Final Solution (cf. 2.1.2.2) finds no reasonable justification, especially for those who managed to survive. Kalowski talks about his life as a son of a helpless father, a victim of war and racial persecution. One example are his memories as a student at a Jewish school where topics like the Holocaust and Nazism were often discussed. Despite those classes, Kalowski, at that age, could not understand the reason for his father's silence and had to learn to accept his father's unwillingness to speak about the Holocaust. In the aftermath of the war, the experience of internment still had its hold on his father's social life. The fellow prisoners he had met in Auschwitz who, like him, had managed to survive, became his only friends. He spent the rest of his life in a sort of parallel world, and was never able to integrate into the local community.

---

[2] "[D]a Auschwitz qualcuno è uscito vivo ma nessuno è sopravvissuto davvero. Queste pagine vogliono essere un omaggio a mio padre e a chi come lui – i più – ha testimoniato con il silenzio l'impossibilità di sgretolare il muro apparso ad un certo punto della sua vita, separandola definitivamente dalla successiva esistenza."

The Nature of Blood depicts this sense of safety among individuals who have experienced the same tragedy. Eva draws comfort from the presence of her mother's ghost:

> Today, Mama arrived back in the camp. At first I was angry, for I thought the person lying in the cot next to me must have broken in during the night in order to steal something. [...] Before I could say anything, the woman turned her face towards me and I saw it was Mama. I wasn't frightened. I was expecting her to return, for I never truly believed that she had gone. And now she is back. I hold her hard and encourage her to tell her story once more. [...] She touches my face as though still unable to believe her luck. [...] I touch my Mama's face, her lips, her eyes, her nose. I stroke her wisps of hair. Mama is back with me. I can now begin to plan a future for both of us. (35-36)

Eva's spends two days secluded in the hut, talking to her mother and planning a future together outside the camp (cf. 2.1.2.3.). To Eva, her mother's presence is so real that she feels compelled to briefly step outside to grab soup for both of them. For survivors accustomed to near starvation conditions in the death camp, food is an obsession. In contrast to the extermination camp, the English soldiers provide for Jewish refugees who, in addition to physical and psychological ailments, are also dealing with "the unbearable pain of hunger" (32). Nonetheless, there is nothing that helps to relieve the pain: "I remain constantly haunted by food. Even though there is plenty to eat, I always carry a piece of bread hidden about me. I am ashamed" (46).
On February 13, 2017, Liliana Segre, a survivor of Shoah, spoke at the University of Turin. At the age of thirteen she was deported to Auschwitz and later transported to Birkenau. For a long time, she had been unable to talk about her experience in those camps, and only in

the nineteen-nineties did she start to reveal what had happened to her. For some years, food became her obsession, and, like Eva, she used to carry with her something to eat when she was outside; while at home, the kitchen was her most frequented room (cf. 2.1.2.2).

The next section will deal with the order of narration in Eva's autobiographical process and her reminiscences of the concentration camp in Bergen-Belsen.

2.1.2.2 Bergen-Belsen

Bergen-Belsen initially was established as an "exchange" or "holding camp." Jews were exchanged for German civilians interned in Allied territory or for hard currency. Along with this type of human trafficking, internees were also subjected to forced labour ("Belsen Concentration Camp"). Although Bergen-Belsen did not contain gas chambers, more than 50,000 people died of starvation, overwork, medical experiments and diseases ("Bergen-Belsen"). On April 15, 1945 British and Canadian troops liberated the camp. In order to prevent the spread of diseases, British soldiers evacuated the camp and burned it down (Ghert-Zand).

In *The Nature of Blood*, Eva and the omniscient narrator do not mention the name of the camp where the Stern family was held in captivity but Bergen-Belsen can be inferred from Phillips's *The European Tribe*, a collection of essays that depict a multiracial Europe of the 1980s. In "Anne Frank's Amsterdam" from that volume Phillips tells of his stopover there; the essay is introduced with a quotation from *The Diary of Anne Frank*:

> *'Then they will find Anne's diary,' added Daddy. 'Burn it then,' suggested the most terrified member of the party. This, and when the police rattled the cupboard door were my worst moments. 'Not my diary, if my diary goes,*

I go with it!' But luckily Daddy didn't answer. (66; emphasis in the original)

This epigraph and allusions to Anne Frank in the essay make a brief comparison between the two young Jewish women seem useful. Anne and Eva are both teenagers and live with their families in a "four-storey house" ("Anne Frank's Amsterdam" 68). When Jews are rounded up and removed to concentration camps, both move to a hiding place to avoid deportation. Both are engaged in personal storytelling: with Anne, the storytelling manifests itself in her diary, whereas in the case of Eva it takes the form of an interior autobiographical process (cf. 2.1.2.1). Nonetheless, there is a difference in the chronological order: Anne writes her diary before her internment, while Eva tells her story afterwards. Anne starts writing her diary to cope with her solitude: "'paper is more patient than man' […] the reason for my starting a diary: it is that I have no such real friend" (Frank 3-4). She shares the experience she is going through with white sheets of paper. Conversely, Eva shows little interest in sharing her thoughts with others. If anything, she looks to erase and escape her memories. She declares more than once that "There is no companionship in despair. […] and I choose to remain alone" (33). However, the sensation of being followed by an imaginary girl compromises Eva's craving for solitude. This perception haunts Eva from the time of her journey from the concentration camp to Cyprus and symbolizes the inescapable personal guilt and shame she carries for being a survivor:

> She followed me across the water. In fact, she follows me everywhere. I have had to learn to tolerate her. I arrive somewhere, then she arrives moments later. I leave for somewhere, then moments later she, too, leaves. At first I used to panic and cry, but she would not listen. […] This was to be a new land, a new beginning. I didn't want her to follow me here. That would not be fair. But

> when we arrived, there she was, dressed in those same rags, standing behind me, waiting for me to decide my next step. Nobody else notices her, even when she tries to reach out and hug me, nobody sees. (196-97)

Despite differences in narration, it can be argued that both Anne's and Eva's narratives function as a relief valve for their painful emotions. The two young women inhabit the same historical reality, they share similar psychological needs along with ways of coping with suffering. *The Nature of Blood* exhibits this connection and the fictitious Eva interacts and sometimes overlaps with the historical figure of Anne.

Based on Phillips's reflections on his stay in Amsterdam, which may be regarded as one of the sources of Eva's story in *The Nature of Blood*, Bénédicte Ledent (156) affirms:

> But Eva's story may puzzle the reader for yet another reason: although it clearly relates to Anne Frank's, it goes beyond the famous diary and projects the young woman's life into a future she never knew. […] as another example of 'misappropriation' on Phillips's part, at the same time, it singularly meets Anne Frank's wish that 'she should go on living even after [her] death' while also soothing Eva's repeated fears of being neither understood nor remembered, thus having her very existence negated.

Ledent's perspective on Eva supports the above-mentioned connection between the two young Jewish women. Giving voice to marginalized individuals, Phillips here acknowledges the female dimension of the persecution of Jews.

Like Anne, who writes "Moreover, according to me, very little progress is being made in the war; in the end the Germans will still win. I'm afraid of our having to starve, and if I'm in a bad mood I scold everyone" (Frank 147), Eva is aware of the horrific reality outside her hiding place. However, perhaps in order to make her concur with Anne Frank's wish – "I want to go on living even after my death!" (Frank 166) – Phillips portrays Eva as a mature and sensible teenager. This is particularly evident in the passage below, specifically in the juxtaposition of "the crumbling buildings" at the time narrated with the prospect of a future without evidence of people like her.

> Here, among these houses which had become our prisons and our tombs, there was no midnight, there were no bells, there was no time. I looked around at the miserable and crumbling buildings, knowing in my heart that those who were hiding would soon be found. And killed. Buildings would be looted, contraband discovered, and whole streets burnt. In time, there would be no evidence that any of us had ever lived here. We never existed. (70-71)

Anne provides details that can applied to Eva's imminent future as well:

> I've only got dismal and depressing news for you today. Our many Jewish friends are being taken away by the dozen. These people are treated by the Gestapo without a shred of decency, being loaded into cattle trucks and sent to Westerbork, the big Jewish camp in Drente. Westerbork sounds terrible: only one washing cubicle for a hundred people and not nearly enough lavatories. [...] Men, women, and children all sleep together. [...] It is impossible to escape; [...] We assume that most of them are murdered. The British radio speaks of their being gassed. Perhaps that is the quickest way to die. (Frank 34-35)

Eva's autobiographical process depicts her secluded life and her "own special pastime" (60) of viewing the world outside:

> First, I would drag a small wooden crate across the floorboards to the window, and then I would mount it so that my chin could rest on the lower sill. From this precarious position, I looked down into the streets. [...] From my perch I observed only bent backs, bare heads and, littering the streets, lonely corpses. [...] I hoped that Mama and Papa's daily search took them to a better place than this, but in my heart I knew otherwise. [...] We knew that everything in our world had changed. In fact, everything in our world was collapsing all about us. (60)

Here Eva witnesses the ongoing ethnic cleansing. Her identification with non-human life forms is expressed by the choice of the word 'perch,' which we tend to associate with birds. Eva is deprived of her status as human being, and, in time, has internalized this animal-like perception of herself. Likewise, she speaks of a "voluntary captivity (for my own safety)" (60), and her desire for life and freedom is represented through far- and fast-travelling birds (cf. 2.1.2.1).

Hitler, in his *Reichstag* speech in January 1939, threatened a world war that would result in the destruction of the Jews in Europe (Browning and Matthäus 425-26). The extermination of the Jews planned and organized by the National Socialist German Workers' Party NSDAP progressed methodically. The efficiency and meticulous record keeping of the Nazi government were such that the likelihood of anyone falling through the cracks of bureaucracy was very low. Jews, like the Sterns, who could afford a hiding place could not escape the grasp of the authorities for long.

The planned extermination was accompanied by a series of psychological and physical acts of violence, each more demeaning and inhumane than the previous. These acts intensify during transportation. Like livestock the deported are crammed together and ultimately treated like inanimate objects deprived of food and water during the journey.

The bewilderment rising from inhumane travel conditions produces a general inability to speak. It is the omniscient narrator's voice that takes over and continues the narration:

> And then she noticed a girl of her own age, perhaps a little older. It was her time of the month, but she could no longer hide the blood. More than any of the others, Eva felt for this girl in her moment of humiliation. Lying in straw sodden with faeces and vomit, all classes and social distinctions had disappeared. (162)

At their destination, the narrator refers to future events – "Only later will they appear in the Register of the Dead. [...] Her name will appear nowhere. Not even counted" (163) – that testify to the systematic approach to exterminate Jews and machine-like relentlessness of the procedure is underscored. The erasure of "all classes and social distinctions" (160) on the trains is followed by the eradication of dignity:

> My hair is removed by a woman who wields large blunt scissors. [...] The hair on my head, the hair under my arms, the soft hair between my legs. [...] Our heads are strange and knobbly. We all look the same. Grotesque figures, naked and without hair. [...] I try to forget my name. I decide to put Eva away in some place for safekeeping until all of this is over. But already Eva refuses

to be hidden. There is no new name in my throat. Eva refuses to disappear. (164)

Perhaps in an attempt to preserve her self-worth, Eva begins to disassociate herself from the grotesque figure she has become. Referring to herself in third person, she determines to resist the erasure of her persona. However, Jews who face up to the realities of life in the camp are "reduced to a small tangle of bones covered with skin that is stretched tight and stained with bruises and bites. Bald heads and powerful eyes" (168). Because of the barbaric treatment, Eva feels that she no longer exists as a material entity: "I have no body. It is my soul that is now being punished" (185). But her determination to resist urges her to warn the newcomers that they "must remember their names. Without a name, nobody will know who they are" (169).

Elias Canetti, in his study on *Crowds and Power*, underscores the importance of one's name: "We can take it for granted that no member of a nation ever sees himself as alone. As soon as he is named, or names himself, something more comprehensive moves into his consciousness, a larger unit to which he feels himself to be related" (Canetti 170). Rendering individuals nameless as it were erases a group.

Eva's "whispered warnings" (168) are a consequence of her traumatic experience in the camp where

> death is a trivial affair. It has become a habit, like the habit of the lice to quarry their way to the armpits. Only typhus is feared, for the head bursts, the body trembles, the intestines and stomach are stricken in agony, leaving one to wallow in pools of excrement of one's own making. The rest is routine. Every day, there are examinations. Men and women in name only. (167-68)

Even though Jews are rendered sexless figures outwardly, "an unaesthetic drop of menstrual blood" (168) still shows "the aggravated abasement that concentration camp life imposes on women," as Ledent (156) points out. The contrast between with a newly arrived pregnant woman, whom Eva helps, and the other female prisoners underscores this:

> (I told her. We were once you. Healthy, with beautiful figures. With long hair. [...] And breasts.) Her full breasts, soon to disappear. An imaginary pebble near the nipple, distorting the length. Then the sack will shrink. Shorter. And then she will become a man. No breasts. (168-69)

The narrator then sums up what will become of them: "Plumes of smoke" (169).

Piecing together Eva's fragmented narration, the reader realizes her secret: she was a member of a *Sonderkommando* during her internment:

> (In the morning, a wealth of corpses. I look and wonder, if I survive, and if I should meet their husbands or children or parents, and if they should ask me about their loved ones, what should I say? Should I confess to the terror in their eyes? Should I say that at some point during these squalid years we all wished to stumble forwards on our swollen feet and simply fall into the ditch. Easy. But to try to survive was terrible. Should I tell them this? That the body begins to eat itself. Fat. Flesh. Muscles. In this order. [...]) [...] (I long for fresh bodies.) [...] (Please do not let me discover anybody that I know.) (167-71)

The last two sentences allude to a cannibalistic practice that is denied. Eva never uses the word *Sonderkommando* in her narrative. Eva is a survivor, maybe because of her work. According to Canetti (228) "the survivor stands in the midst of the fallen. For him there is one tremendous fact: while countless others have died, many of them his comrades, he is still alive." To survive, as it were, means living to the detriment of the other. Canetti (468) goes further and states that surviving is a dark, sinful deed, therefore "The survivor is mankind's worst evil, its curse and perhaps its doom." This explains the survivors' sense of shame, guilt and, perhaps, their inability to give information, to express his/her experience in words. Silence shelters the survivor from questions, because, as Canetti points out,

> Questions are intended to be answered; those which are not answered are like arrows shot into the air. The most innocuous questions are those which remain isolated and do not lead on to others. […] Sometimes, however, the questioner is not content with this and will put further questions. […] every answer he receives is an act of submission. Personal freedom consists largely in having a defence against questions. The most blatant tyranny is the one which asks the most blatant questions. (Canetti 285)

Silence as a form of protection from further acts of violence (i.e. questions) becomes synonymous with freedom, a form of redemption from further subjugation.

Despite the suffering the recollection of past events may cause, Eva speaks about her *Sonderkommando* work:

> Today, they continue to burn bodies. (I burn bodies.) Burning bodies. First, she lights the fire. Pour gasoline, make a torch, and then ignite the pyre. Wait for the explosion as the fire catches, and then wait for the smoke. (170)

In this memory in the form of a sort of checklist the repetition of "burn bodies," strengthened by alliteration, suggests a procedure through which death becomes "routine" (168).

Eva describes this routine thus:

> Every day, there are exterminations. [...] (Before I work I need food.) A piece of bread is a lifeline. [...] Lick your spoon. Lick your spoon. No clock. No time. Now only work. March to work. [...] And again the moon. (I look at the moon. Still pregnant. Every month pregnant.) Standing in line with people with big heads, and within their big heads only the eyes are living. Always the eyes. A piece of black bread, four inches thick. Whispering. Bread? More bread? [...] Don't get sick. It is evening. [...] Rats feed on human bodies. Dead or alive. The distinction is irrelevant. (168-71)

The caring, maternal recommendation, "Don't get sick," encourages resistance to the unbelievable and shocking reality that has become her life in the camp. Due to the absence of clocks, watching the moon becomes Eva's method for measuring time and it indicates her determination to resist, at least on a psychological level, the erasure of her female physical characteristics. The association of the full moon with pregnancy could be taken to represent Eva's hope for a future life outside the camp. However, given what the omniscient narrator tells us, that goal hardly seems achievable. Detainees face starvation, as mentioned above the constant feeling of hunger persists after their release.

Maybe deliberately, Eva herself does not provide a clear definition of her role in the *Sonderkommando*. As usual, the cruel reality of how the "process of gassing takes place" is brought out by the omniscient narrator's voice (176-77).

Zygmunt Bauman (13) conceives of the Holocaust as one of the "products of civilization." The Nazi mass murder took the shape of "a factory-produced vehicle, wielding weapons only the most advanced science could supply, and following an itinerary designed by scientifically managed organization. [...] It was the rational world of modern civilization that made the Holocaust thinkable."

As a feature of modern civilization, the Holocaust necessarily is subject to bureaucracy. The painstakingly accurate record keeping and the accompanying medical and scientific research show discipline and dedication to a cause, an ideal, a target to achieve in order to enhance human beings' existence. The general population was manipulated to accept the racial ideology of the Nazis as a benefit for German society, which was hardly directly affected by the fighting during World War I. Hitler aspired to a Nazi-dominated Europe. Differently from previous forms of imperialism based on economic and political domination, Nazi ideology additionally was built on the concept of racial supremacy and the goal of a *judenfrei* Germany was at the core of the Final Solution (Bauman 14-18).

2.1.2.3 London

> SUICIDE: An act of voluntary and intentional self-destruction. St Thomas Aquinas (1225-74) claimed that suicide was a mortal sin because it usurped God's power over human life and death. However, neither the Old nor the New Testament directly forbids suicide.
> – Phillips (*Nature* 185)

In order to highlight the connections between what appear to be fragmented stories in *The Nature of Blood*, I will focus on the last part of Eva's autobiographical process in this section. So far it has been established that the narrative starts in Cyprus, where a profoundly traumatized Eva meets Gerry, an English soldier.

Eva's voice slips into the narration anonymously. Her voice comments on a Cypriot moment: "I WATCH as the trucks come roaring into the camp, dust and mud flying up behind their wheels. As the men jump down to the ground, they whistle and shout to each other" (12). Instead of beginning with basic introductory details such as name, age, provenance, Eva starts her narrative depicting the arrival of lively, boisterous young men: "These English men have arrived on this warm spring day and now we are free" (12). The information provided by the narrating voices earlier suggests a note of irony in Eva's use of the word "free." Undoubtedly, the Jews concerned are now "free" from Nazi persecution, but it is only freedom in name, as they are still held in detention camps, this time on the island of Cyprus.

Immediately after the end of World War II, Great Britain, to which Palestine had been mandated at the conference of San Remo (1920), imposed restrictive immigration quotas in Palestine for Jews. This fact is mentioned by Stephan: "the British quota of seven hundred and fifty persons per month meant that thousands would have to spend weeks, if not years, under British lock and key on Cyprus" (5).

> Luckily [Jews] seemed to understand that here, on Cyprus, the British were not the enemy. These reluctant soldiers were captors. They inflicted no punishment, and there was neither torture nor killing. The British were bored. Bored with their Mr Bevin, bored with Cyprus, bored with Jews. They couldn't care less about breaking the power of the 'Hebrew Resistance Movement'. The war was over and they wanted to go home. (7-8)

Although Eva is aware of these differences between the time when the Nazis held sway and her present circumstances, she cannot help but view the behaviour of the British as that of captors and finds parallels between the camps of the two powers. The repetition of the experience as captive is commented on as follows: "A doctor inspects my tufts of hair. A nurse cuts them off. Again, a factory line. Again, we are being processed. But this time for life. (Apparently, I weigh sixty pounds.) They give me women's clothing" (19).

In contrast to her disjointed narrative, Eva's behaviour on the Mediterranean island is stable and consistent. She prefers to keep aloof from other human beings, even if her efforts are not entirely successful. For instance, when she is still new in the camp and spends her time warily observing and taking in her physical environment, the protective wall of her solitude begins to reveal tiny cracks and slowly the presence of other human beings begins to slip through those cracks: "the man comes to me. [...] He looks young. In fact, not much older than I am. He offers me [...] a piece of chocolate [...] And then he stands back [...] unsure of what to do next" (13). The man's first hesitant approach affects Eva's desire to be left alone. She informs us of another attempt on his part that occurs

> from the side. I cannot see him, for I am sitting outside the hut and resting my back up against the wall. [...]. I do not wish to see anything or anybody.
> [...]
> There is a long silence, which I imagine will be resolved only if I turn to look at this man.
> [...]
> 'I'm Gerry. From London.'
> 'Hello, Gerry.'
> Already I have progressed too far.
> 'Hello,' he laughs. 'What's your name?'
> This is enough. Gerry does not understand. I cannot possibly travel at the speed of this Gerry. (18-19)

Despite Eva's insistent reluctance, Gerry slowly succeeds in setting up a communication channel. In the subsequent encounters, he strategically initiates the conversation by offering some food (23) which functions as a magnet for a survivor who experienced starvation.

However, Gerry's kindness arouses suspicion: "His attention, while flattering, also causes me to worry. I decide that, in future, I will avoid this man as much as possible" (21). But Eva cannot avoid him and ultimately reveals her name and intention of finding her sister. Gerry, who entirely adheres to his role of liberator, offers his help. Then, before leaving the camp for London, as a sign of farewell, he also gives Eva some money as well as his address:

> 'Please, take it. You have to get used to doing normal things again.'
> For a brief second I hate Gerry. How dare he talk to me about normal? About what I have to do. I do not have to do anything that I do not want to do. He has no idea of what is normal and what is not normal.
> [...]
> I look again at Gerry. Then at the money in his hand. He is trying to buy my affection. But if I am to find my sister, I need this man's help. I take the money.
> [...]
> 'I have the address of your D.P.[3] And here, this is for you.'
> He holds out a piece of paper that is folded over twice, as though containing a secret.
> 'My address in London,' he says. He appears to be beaming with pride. 'You must write to me if you need anything. Otherwise I'll write to you.'
> He pauses and looks around himself.
> 'You should come to London. I think you'd like it.'

---

[3] After being freed by the Allied armies the survivors were sent to D.P. (displaced persons) camps, where they could be processed, their identities filed and, when possible, reunited with their families.

I smile, and wonder just what it is that Gerry imagines makes this London so special.
'Here, take it.'
He thrusts the piece of paper towards me.
'Thank you, Gerry.'
'Don't thank me,' he says. 'Not till you've made use of it.' (30-42)

In this passage, Eva dwells on Gerry's inability to comprehend her psychological state, but above all, she needs a plausible answer to the question that continuously obsessed Jewish people during the Nazi regime: "How is it possible to be so angry with people who have done you no wrong?" (93). Eva does not need to be questioned. The idea of providing private details of her life to a foreigner, especially one "dressed in a heavy khaki uniform" (13), is a reminder of Nazi bureaucratic procedure and violence perpetrated against Jewish civilians. As Canetti reminds us, questions are another form of violence. The fact that some questions have no answers accounts for and justifies the silence that characterizes survivors as well as witnesses of atrocity (cf. 2.1.2.2).

Trauma causes a void in time and this "implies a disturbed relationship between the world, the self, and representation, and points to the crisis of referentiality. This renders the linear narrative with causal and chronological links between events impossible" (Osman 161). These effects of trauma are mirrored in Eva's narrative as informed by her fragile psychological state.

Eva's admission that she "cannot possibly travel at the speed of this Gerry" (19) is another indication of trauma. According to Khan Touseef Osman (160), "trauma involves a rupture in the temporal and symbolic orders at individual levels." This rupture, along with the defensive amnesia, leads to a fragmented sense of time, which is reflected in the novel's narrative structure. Our effort to fill the gaps between the interrupted storylines resembles the effort that Eva has to make to overcome trauma, even though the act of pulling herself together is a slower, incomparably more arduous process. The traumatized Eva, in the attempt to react, recounts her life events relying on a narrative that is characterized by the employment of devices such as repetition, the figure of the ghost – her "Mama" (13; cf. 2.1.2.1) and the imaginary girl who "followed her across the water" (196; cf. 2.1.2.2) – and the absence of chronological order.

Eva is the only survivor of her family and feels imprisoned in her sense of isolation. If, on the one hand, she opts to remain apart from others as a self-defence mechanism to avoid questions, on the other hand, she is pleased by Gerry's attention. This contradiction highlights Eva's ambivalence towards others. In regard to the ambivalent character of Eva, Ledent (*Caryl Phillips* 157) states, "Phillips depicts an Eva who is all the more human for her imperfection. Not only is she prejudiced towards 'the dirty, uncultivated people from the east' (169), but she is also able, out of despair, to forge a letter of proposal that she signs with Gerry's own name."

In Cyprus Gerry bids farewell to Eva, adhering to his role of liberator. Gerry's "leaving present" (33) of money is intended to allow Eva "to get used to doing normal things again" (30). Eva realizes that the money indicates his departure; this means an end to the attention paid to her by the English soldier who opened a window to an imaginary, more agreeable existence for Eva, one where Gerry proposes to her:

> 'When you come to London, will you marry me?'
> He pauses as though his own words have shocked him to his core. As the silence deepens, I can see that he desperately needs me to rescue him.
> 'Gerry,' I begin.
> 'Eva.' He pauses. 'When you're better, of course. Will you marry me?' (42-43)

Eva holds on to this imaginary proposal and, unlike the other women from the camp who "are making nervous plans. For Palestine" (44), she plans to escape solitude by seeking out Gerry in England: "Tomorrow, I leave for England and Gerry. [...] Tomorrow, they will release me into an empty world with only Gerry for company" (47-48).

The Nazis stripped the Jews of all their assets. This violent removal also triggered a sense of emotional deprivation. Nonetheless, in Cyprus, the Jewish detainees

> speak with a sudden and miraculous energy [...] Apparently, [they] have wandered long enough. [They] have worked and struggled too long on the lands of other peoples. The journey that [they] are making across the bones of Europe is a story that will be told in future years by many prophets. After hundreds of years of trying to be with others, of trying to be others, [they] are now pouring in the direction of home. (44-45)

Like other liberated Jewish survivors of the camps, Eva too wants to go home, but her idea of home is not connected to Palestine and echoes Robert Frost's suggestion: "Home is the place where, when you have to go there, they have to take you in" (Phillips, *New World Order* 303). Somehow she develops a personal concept of home that is dissociated from blood ties and/or nationality. As a matter of fact, she defines home a locus where she is received with pleasure and hospitality. Rather than to a physical site, the idea of home is attached to human beings; home can be anywhere:

> 'Are you waiting for anybody from home?'
> Stupid woman. Waiting where? Who knows where I am.
> I am not sure myself. I refuse to speak.
> 'Do you intend to go home?'

How can she use the word 'home'? It is cruel to do so in such circumstances. I cannot call that place 'home'. 'Home' is a place where one feels a welcome. (36-37)

Eva's opinion that home is "where one feels welcome" has been reached, as Ledent (157) points out, "out of despair" and, like the Windrush generation in the forties, she identifies home with London. The motive for such conviction is that "Gerry's letter said come to England. He said he still wanted to marry me. He could not find Margot, but he said we could make a new life together. And so I boarded a train that furrowed its slow way across Europe towards the English Channel" (188-89).

As a Jew, Eva again makes "a journey [...] across the bones of Europe" (45) but this time "pouring in the direction of home" (45). However, like the colonized people who feel they belong to their "mother country" and expect to be accepted but are not, in London Eva feels unwanted, as when she comments on a taxi driver: "He looks at me with an invitation to leave his taxi. To leave his city. To leave his country" (189).

At this point, it may be useful to introduce Sean Purchase's ideas on the notion of "mother country" in the context of the British Empire. As emerges from the stories narrated in the novel, England participates in the fragmented sequence of history featuring a sort of "almighty"/steady presence. The image of Britain as the mother country was introduced during the reign of Queen Victoria, when the British Empire reached its maximum expansion. In this context, Purchase points out that 'family' is one of the key words associated with the Victorian Age: family became the core of that new political and territorial unit, with children gaining importance within family and society at large. According to Purchase, the Victorian concept of childhood "links the idea of childhood to another form of wild or rather 'primitive' innocence in British consciousness: the 'noble savage.'"[4] At the encounter with the "Other" in the Americas, British colonists and anthropologists coined the term 'noble savage.' Through this coinage, the subjugator established that the differences in customs and practices were due to the native peoples' "primitive" innocence. The labelling as noble savage attributed an infantile state to these "uncivilized" peoples, allowing the colonizer to regard them as stemming from the "childhood of humanity."

If, at the beginning, the treatment of the colonized people at times seemed "paternal," it soon revealed itself as an instrument to camouflage the true purpose of the imperial project, namely the oppression and exploitation of colonized peoples. In that imperial context, where family represented the framework of Victorian society, both inside and outside the island, in order to justify its presence and its function as bearer of culture and civilization, Britain developed into the figure of the "mother country" that nurtured the "childhood" of humanity. Consequently, as in the familial bond between a mother and her offspring, the language spoken by the parent became the mother-tongue of the British Empire (Purchase 17). This brief explanation will be drawn upon in the following sections.

No sooner has Eva arrived at Gerry's house than she discovers that he is married and has a child. Eventually, Gerry shows up and instead of exhibiting pleasure at seeing her, he takes Eva to a pub:

> 'The wife. Well, I told her you were a bit crackers. I'm sorry, but I had to tell her something.' Please, Gerry, do not do this to me. Do not be somebody else now that you are back home. […] I don't want to be hurt again. I won't be able to survive being abandoned again. Not

---

[4] According to Purchase, the idea of the child as the "purest" stage of human development has its roots in the eighteenth century, in so far as the romantic pastoral image of the child may be connected to the beginning of the Industrial Revolution, a process that began in England from about 1760 and modified both social order and landscape.

again. [...] I realized that Gerry had probably said all that he was going to say to me. I watched him now, laughing with his friend at the bar. No, Gerry. No. Surely you are better than this? (194)

The shock of suddenly being confronted by reality causes Eva to lose her memory, and only at the hospital (an insane asylum) does a doctor explain her condition to her. She plunges into aphasia. The disorder becomes a shelter for her solitude. Her abdication of spoken language is then expressed on various occasions in her narrative:

But last night, in the pub, I finally abandoned words [...] I remember that I do not talk. (Last night, in the pub, I finally abandoned words.) [...] 'Why did you write the letter, Eva? Mr Alston. I mean, Gerry. He has a wife and child. As you can imagine, this has caused him some difficulties.' He takes his hands from mine. 'Did you write the letter so that you might prove something to somebody, is that it?' He does not seem to understand that I do not talk. Last night, in the pub, I finally abandoned words. (190-96)

Even though she has renounced words, she remains dedicated to carrying on with her autobiographical process. She describes Gerry's visit and finally admits having signed the letter with his name.

Perhaps as a gesture of common courtesy, Gerry brings her "a chocolate cake, and a knife with which to cut it" (197). This encounter puts an end not only to their relationship but also to Eva's existence. It may be argued that the chocolate, mentioned on the first and the last occasion when Gerry and Eva are together (13, 187), symbolizes the frame that encapsulates Gerry and Eva's fragmented story.

The psychiatrist attending to Eva admits that he was out of his depth with this patient:

> *She wasn't considered to be a serious problem. There were no seizures or fits. But, sadly, we were wrong. There was a problem. There was also a lot of blood. She cut the right artery, as though she knew what she was doing. A lot of blood.* (186; emphasis in the original)

By contrast, a clearheaded Eva concludes her narrative with precise words:

> I know that somewhere, buried deep inside me, is a place where I will be able to lay down in peace. […] But until then? Can I ever be truly happy? […] Mama. Papa. I do not know in what strange land you are buried. Or what stubbled growth or building defaces the earth above your precious bones. But I am tired. And I want to come home. […] Mama. Papa. Dear Margot. […] Everything will be fine. Please. Don't worry. (198)

The Nature of Blood being rooted in the Anglophone postcolonial novel tradition, Eva's suicide in London, at the heart of the Empire, also suggests death at a larger scale: it may refer to the victims of colonialism, or to the fall of the British Empire. The "mother country," conveyor of culture, education and civilization to overseas peoples considered inferior, is not able to nurture them when they arrive in the country they define as home.

2.1.3 Malka

> *My sister and I wondered, in this new land, would our babies be born white? We, the people of the House of Israel, we were going home. No more wandering. No*

> *longer landless. No more tilling of soil that did not belong to us.*
> – Caryl Phillips (*Nature* 201; emphasis in the original)

The Ethiopian Malka belongs to a large cast of minor characters in *The Nature of Blood*. She is introduced by the omniscient narrator as we approach the last pages of the novel:

> HE had been watching her for a long time. She sat alone across the room, her face an impassive mask, while the other women swirled and dipped in large gestures of exaggerated joy. [...] but this woman was beautiful. He could not take his eyes from her. [...] but this woman, who nobody asked to dance, simply sat as though she was indifferent to people's attitudes towards her. Once more, the music stopped and partners were hastily exchanged, and he watched as, again, this woman was ignored. (198-99)

The person staring at her is the aged Stephan. At this point in the novel, he has managed to settle in the "promised land" and, having recently retired from his medical profession, has begun to feel increasingly lonely. On Wednesday afternoons, as a way to relieve the weight of solitude, he frequents a club where underpaid young women – "prostitutes, [...] students, or unemployed actresses" (199) – offer male customers "their weekly flights of fantasy" (199). The omniscient narrator goes on to describe how Stephan approaches this woman. Delineating Stephan's reaction to solitude (cf. 2.1.1), the narrator gives further details from her conversation with Stephan which takes place as she dutifully dances with him: "After her arrival, she had undergone two years of intensive language study, and then she had trained as a nurse. However, at present she was not working. She would say nothing more" (200). In contrast to her reluctance to converse with Stephan, she liberally narrates her story in interior monologues.

These also provide political and historical information. Malka's soliloquies differ from the other stories in the novel in that they are presented in italics, which underscores the recurring nature of certain historical events.

Before revealing her name, the woman describes how she and others were transported like livestock: *"And then you herded us on to buses. Relatives were being abandoned. And then on to the embassy compound, where we were stored like thinning cattle* (199; emphasis in the original). The people addressed as "you" here are self-proclaimed purveyors of culture and civilization for people regarded as uncivilized, even as lacking fully human status. In the specific context of Israel and African Jews, despite the fact that both groups have the same religion, the airlifting of Ethiopian Jews is another instance of hierarchical relationships between whites and non-whites (cf. 2.2).

One disturbing aspect of the transportation is its selective and discriminatory nature: *"Not everybody was here. It was impossible to take everybody. Relatives were being abandoned. […] I was lucky, for my parents, and my brother and sister, were relatively healthy* (199; emphasis in the original). The selection process is based on market and profit priorities. The healthy, if "inferior," persons considered suitable for inclusion in the "chosen people" are selected by "superior" beings according to criteria determined by the latter.

Resuming the story of her flight, the woman tells of her fears on the plane which, however, are mitigated by her arrival in *"Zion"* (200), her people's home. It is at this point in the narration that she finally tells the reader her name, Malka. The fact that this revelation coincides with her arrival in Israel suggests that escaping Ethiopia has had a liberating effect on her: the disclosure of her identity is connected to Israel, the historical land of the Jewish people. As black Jews, who experienced exclusion and marginalization in Ethiopia, the newcomers are now part of the "chosen people" after centuries of exile.

The omniscient narrator adds further details: Stephan is attracted to Malka but unable to engage in a conversation that would lead them to a more intimate relationship: "She refused to be any more specific with regard to her domestic arrangements" (202). Nevertheless, her renewed marginalization in Israel emerges from what she does say about herself: she and her family live "at the edge of the city in one of the developments into which her people had been placed" (202).

Malka's last soliloquy expresses a severe criticism of her white "brothers and sisters":

> *(This Holy Land did not deceive us. The people did. The man at the hostel, he said to us, 'Welcome, my black brothers and sisters. You are helping us to understand what we are doing here.' Is this true? Are we helping you? I know now what a stamp is. I can use a telephone. I, too, can turn night into day by simply pressing a switch. I wear shoes. I have seen a highway. But please. My people never killed themselves. Hunger, yes. Disease, yes. But never this problem. During Passover, we kill a lamb and sprinkle its fresh red blood around the synagogue. But not here. You do not allow this. You say you rescued me. Gently plucked me from one century, helped me to cross two more, and then placed me in this time. Here. Now. But why? What are you trying to prove?)*
> (207-08; emphasis in the original)

The Ethiopian Jews' relocation in the "promised land" duplicates another displacement. The plucking talked about in the above passage recalls the slave trade. As Africans, the Ethiopian Jews are considered inferior, a sentiment expressed by Stephan a few pages later, when he speaks of "dragging these people from their primitive world into this one" (210). The building of a society from the "chosen people" has failed. It should have been a society based on religion, where "brothers and sisters" were not discriminated by the colour of their skin. Commenting on Stephan's words, Ledent (140) points out that in the long term feelings of racism towards the "Other" arise unavoidably. Likewise, according to Isabelle Hesse (896), "Phillips shows that any form of belonging always results in the majority creating a social hierarchy, which [as a consequence] excludes the minority."

It may be worth remarking on a recent manifestation of fear of miscegenation. In 2013, global headlines reported that the Israeli government had applied birth control to African immigrants without their consent. Ethiopian women were, in effect, subjected to forced sterilization (Knutsen) – a clear parallel to the forced sterilization of slaves in the USA. Instances like this bear out Phillips attempt to show how equality, freedom and justice are denied to doubly-diasporic people like Malka who inhabits the intersection between Jewish and African diasporas.

2.2 The Jewish Question

> Is Europe any different? And that super-European monstrosity, North America? Chatter, chatter: liberty, equality, fraternity, love, honour, patriotism, and what have you. All this did not prevent us from making anti-racial speeches about dirty niggers, dirty Jews, and dirty Arabs. Highminded people, liberal or just softhearted, protest that they were shocked by such inconsistency; but they were either mistaken or dishonest, for with us there is nothing more consistent than a racist humanism *since the European has only been able to become a man through creating slaves and monsters.*
> – Jean-Paul Sartre (preface in Fanon, *Wretched* 25-26; emphasis mine)

The triangular trade involving Europe, Africa and North America that triggered the African diaspora is a central and recurring concern of Phillips's novels. The new element in Phillips's treatment in *The Nature of Blood* is that here the tips of the triangular narrative are pointing to Europe, Africa and, not North America, but the Middle East and the Jewish diaspora. He shifts his focus from the Atlantic Ocean to the Mediterranean Sea, but a different scenario does not necessarily imply different actors.

In the early twentieth century, the British Empire's expansionist ambitions are threatened by the emerging powers of the United States and Germany. This menace to the Empire's dominant status lies behind Britain's increased involvement in the Middle East. After World War I Palestine was put under British tutelage until it was able to govern itself, but, as history demonstrated in the two decades that followed, Great Britain played an ambivalent role in the newly annexed Middle Eastern territory. The British government alternatively aided the causes of Arabs and Zionist activists to preserve its colonial interests. Direct and indirect reflections of this in *The Nature of Blood*, are particularly present in the sections dedicated to Stephan and Eva and highlighted in the present analysis.

Phillips uses the triangular framework to examine the different aspects of physical, social and mental space, the latter being inhabited by memory and the awareness of one's individual and historical Jewish origins. Far from converging harmoniously, the three elements of this tripartite structure clash and cause a feeling of displacement among the diaspora. Each character in the novel has a personal, idealized concept of home that sometimes resembles a utopian fantasy. As mentioned earlier, Stephen Howe claims that African diasporic people envisioned home, i.e. Africa, as a bucolic place (cf. 2.1.1). This romanticization of home is already apparent in the first lines of the novel when Stephan describes the "promised land" to Moshe, another resident of the detainment camp in Cyprus:

> 'Tell me, what will be the name of the country?'
> Israel. Palestine. [...] 'The fruit is on the trees. You may take it straight from the branch.' Moshe looked up at me as though I were holding something back; as though there were some awful secret about this *imaginary country* that I was refusing to share with him. [...] But I was hiding nothing from Moshe. [...]
> 'You will marry a beautiful girl and have wonderful children.' [...] Fruit on the trees. An army. Beautiful women. A new country to build. After two months in Cyprus, I was leaving at dawn. To go home. To go where? Away to the south. Away to the east. How much should I tell this boy? Truly I felt ashamed, for I had not described my country. *I had described the country that might be his. The country that might belong to his children. The country that might belong to his children's children.* [...] I have encouraged my young Moshe to think only of the future. [...] Tell me, what will be the

name of the country? A good question. A fine question. It is difficult for me. My mind is tormented. *You will marry a beautiful girl and have wonderful children. Israel. Moshe, think only of the future.* My young friend, Moshe. (3-12; emphasis mine)

In sharp contrast to Stephan's rosy depiction of Israel, for some characters the country offers a very different reality. The "promised land," it turns out, is a place where certain categories of Jews are excluded, marginalized and subjected to prejudice on the grounds of their skin colour as we learn from Malka's soliloquies:

In our country, we were not used to relying on outsiders. [...] Have you seen the ugly housing at the edges of the city where we live? [...] After the absorption centre, [my parents] are frightened of white walls and white coats. They simply watch television. My mother is tattooed on her face, her hands and her neck. She finds it difficult to leave the apartment, for people stop and stare. (207; emphasis in the original)

Eva and Malka's reflections further convey dissimilar, very personal ideas of home. As pointed out in the previous section, after her traumatic experience in the Nazi concentration camp, Eva develops a concept of home as a place where the individual is welcome (36-37). Home is not necessarily associated with religion, blood kinship or the "promised land." However, before committing suicide, a weary Eva expresses her need to go home and now, unlike previously, the place she identifies with feeling welcome and safe is her family, her blood kinship: "Mama. Papa. Dear Margot" (198; cf. 2.1.2.3). Transferred to "Zion," Malka develops a longing for her village in Ethiopia (207).

In her soliloquies, where at times she cannot help but question the "superior" culture and civilization of the white man, Malka draws our attention to the irony running through this idealistic plan for re-uniting the white and black siblings of Israel. For all its optimistic promise of a country that belongs equally to all Jews, the dominant white Jewish society replicates the racist view towards its darker-skinned citizens evident in European colonies in Africa.

In his introduction (xii) to Joseph Conrad's *Heart of Darkness* (1899), Phillips describes the novel as "an ironic tale of rescue that contains a powerful meditation on the relationship between 'civilization' and 'barbarity.'" In his own work, Phillips underscores the stark contrast between actual and intended achievements in the white European bearer of culture and civilization to the "primitive" peoples of Africa. This is what Malka does in *The Nature of Blood*. The black Jewish woman seems to epitomize all the minority groups that throughout history have been striving against injustice and discrimination in Western white societies.

Particularly relevant is Phillips's (xiii) comment on "the greater horror of recognizing how quickly the benevolence of European colonization can corrode into European criminality, and how quickly man's capacity for evil can rise from beneath the paper-thin veneer of European 'civilization.'" This consideration regarding his reading of *Heart of Darkness* remains valid in Malka's story. To begin with, Malka represents a disquieting encounter with the "Other." She finds herself adrift in situations that challenge her life values and religious beliefs. Though she acknowledges the so-called civilized manners and practices she had to adapt to in the "promised land" – "*I can use a telephone. [...] I wear shoes. I have seen a highway*" (207) –, she does not overlook the fact that the use of scientific knowledge to make Western life easier has not overcome violence. On this topic of violence, she exposes an evident paradox. During Passover, the Jews of European origin, carriers of a white colonial culture and history, do not allow their black siblings to sacrifice lambs in gratitude for their liberation (208). As Malka remarks, during their exile in Ethiopia black Jews died only of poor life conditions. By contrast, their white siblings in Israel still perpetrate violence against their Arab neighbours in the name of defending the "promised land," which might be a reference to terrorist attacks by Jewish paramilitary groups (cf. 2.1.1).

The encounter with the stranger arouses mistrust. Ryszard Kapuściński (9-11) attempts to explain this reaction providing a personal definition of the "Other," of an individual or group that is in some way unlike "us." Aware of the various meaning of the phrase 'the Other,' Kapuściński is careful to employ the term very broadly to distinguish between Western, white Europeans and non-white, non-Europeans. He argues that members of the human race have, in addition to biological traits, also a cultural and a racial identity which depends upon various variables that may range from surrounding context, expectations to age as well as attitude. More often than not, intercultural and inter-racial contact, instead of stimulating curiosity and openness, give rise to prejudice and withdrawal. Anyone who is not identified as belonging to "us" can be addressed as the "Other" indistinctly.

Kapuściński's reflections are borne out by Igiaba Scego's novel *Adua* (2015), which describes the cultural alienation of Somalis living in Italy from the nineteen-thirties to the present. The alienated Zoppe finds shelter from the racism he suffers as a dark-skinned African in his visions and reminisces on his past life in Somalia but also on his present life in Rome where a local Jewish family welcome him in their house:

> It was incredible for him to see white Jews. Zoppe had known only Falasha Jews, the Beta Israel, from Lake Tana, even though his father had told him that in the West there were Jews 'with skin as pale as the moon.' These were pink Jews, so cordial, and their Roman house so cosy and inviting. (Scego, trans. Richards 36)[5]

---

[5] Era stata tanta la meraviglia di vedere degli ebrei bianchi. Zoppe aveva conosciuto solo gli ebrei falascià, i Beta Israel, del lago Tana, anche se il padre gli aveva

This passage from Scego's novel exemplifies the general disposition described by Kapuściński to blindly rely on one's own culture's perspective. Perhaps, as Kapuściński surmises, this is a consequence of humankind's disposition to being sedentary. If not driven by curiosity, human beings tend to settle in one place and limit their exchanges with the outside world. When a journey is undertaken, it is often out of desperation or fear, during a time of religious, ethnic, political or economic strife, for example. In circumstances of heightened anxiety, where personal or group survival are seen as threatened, the unknown "Other" may be perceived as a menace and will tend to evoke feelings of aversion and hostility (*L'altro* 14).

As soon as the "Other" – *nolens volens* – takes up residence in the host nation, irreconcilable diversities among the host and guest societal groups emerge. These differences are enlisted to legitimize hierarchies within which the "Other"/newcomer is inevitably placed at a lower rung on the social ladder.

The relationship with the "Other" is at the core of post- and neo-colonial Anglophone literature. Novels that belong to this genre often address the issues of cohabitation between different ethnic groups and the marginalization experienced by non-whites. Although *The Nature of Blood* belongs to this genre, Phillips provides a modification to traditional post-colonial presentations of the "Other." In the Eurocentric Western collective consciousness the diasporic Jew is white. Phillips seemingly adapts to this general tendency when he introduces, for the first time in his fiction, a white diasporic figure. In this way he expands our very arbitrary view of migrants and of the "Other." However, having thus broadened our notion of outsider/"Other" to include groups which are clearly white to European eyes, Phillips then reshuffles the categories by introducing the black Jew and an emphasis on prejudice based on skin complexion. Through Malka, Phillips gives

---

raccontato che in Occidente esistevano ebrei 'dalla pelle candida come la luna.' Questi ebrei rosa, così cordiali, e la loro casa romana così piccola e accogliente. (Scego 36)

voice to the outcast within the Jewish ethnic group in which religion should function as a bond. We thus become aware of the Ethiopian black Jews' unequal status. From Malka's narrative we learn that their discrimination begins immediately upon arrival in the "promised land." The white Jews impose their language and educational system on the newcomers as a first step in the integration process: *"First we will teach you the language, then when you leave the absorption centre you will be able to study at the university"* (207). This phase of transition represents yet another instance of white "saviours" asserting their authority over their darker complexioned fellow members of the "chosen people." Behind a surface of welcoming home the black siblings of Israel lies the intent to adapt them to the white siblings' rules, societal system and culture.

A look at Foucault's views on education will be instructive in this context. Foucault provides a more sombre view on the matter than his predecessors writing on education. He regards knowledge as a tool of control. Foucault questions our Western civilization and authorities' often insatiable tendency to exercize power in every sphere of individuals' life. According to Foucault, the adjective 'disciplinary' defines a type of "knowledge [that is] used to monitor, classify, and control individuals through techniques that take away individuals' ability to choose for themselves, and which turn them into an object known and controlled by others" (Miller 9). The "mother country" rhetoric of colonial Britain, which imposed its language and education on subjugated peoples overseas is an example of this controlling ideology.

Phillips's novel *Cambridge* illustrates such acculturating of colonized peoples. In the novel, the slave Cambridge speaks to us eloquently, when on the last day of his life, he recounts his existence, including two hellish sojourns in slave ships:

> Pardon the liberty I take in unburdening myself with these hasty lines, but thanks be to God for granting me powers of self-expression in the English language. I

humbly beg that those of my dear England, Africans of my own complexion, and *creoles* of both aspects, might bear with me as I attempt to release from within my person the nature of my extraordinary circumstances. (*Cambridge* 133; emphasis in the original)

Cambridge depicts the colonizers as characterized by "cursed avidity for wealth" from which result "cruelty, knavery, and practice of diabolical arts by English navigators that has turned the hearts of my simple people from natural goodness, and honest affection, towards acts of abomination" (133). Cambridge's superior ability to articulate his reflections made possible by his British education raises him to a level equal to that of his colonial masters but it does not protect him from humiliation and being hanged because of his skin colour. Ledent (99) summarizes this paradox of sharing a language while being marginalized through that same language as "colonized by language, and excluded by language."

Another example of purported integration through language is provided by Ngũgĩ wa Thiong'o. In his memoir *In the House of the Interpreter* (2012), wa Thiong'o describes the nineteen-fifties in Kenya, a country under a state of emergency in response to the Mau Mau rebellion against British rule. wa Thiong'o attends an *élite* English school that aims at turning out "civic-minded blacks who would work within the parameters of the existing racial state" (10). He realizes that the "physical violence of the battlefield" has shifted into "the psychological violence of the classroom" (wa Thiong'o, *Decolonising* 9), exemplified, for instance, in the teaching of African history from an imperialist viewpoint. wa Thiong'o's critical thinking makes him realize that none of the subjects taught in school "reflected [his] black experience" (*House* 162) and that "the language of [his] education was no longer the language of [his] culture" (*Decolonising* 11).

As pointed out earlier, in *The Nature of Blood*, Malka manifests bewilderment every time she attempts to understand the culture of her white Israeli fellow citizens, a culture she has to adapt to even though it often clashes with her values and beliefs. In order to illustrate what I perceive to be one of Phillips's aims – drawing parallels among ruling powers that over centuries have subjugated peoples – I would like to use the example of the imposition of a foreign language and culture from Andrea Levy's *Small Island*.

In this novel, as in Malka's story, the use of the common language as a means of enforcing subservience in colonized peoples is a central topic. Malka does not represent the traditional figure of the colonized individual in that she has been transferred to "Zion," her ancestors' religious home. And yet, the state treats her as a colonized individual. She has to learn the language of the ruling power. In both cases (Malka and Hortense, the Jamaican character in *Small Island*) language functions as a tool for exerting control. The official reason the state gives for its mission to teach newcomers the host language is to facilitate integration and improve job opportunities which, in both novels, never materialize. If immigrants do not benefit from learning English or Hebrew, respectively, the host state clearly does, because having newcomers understand rules makes life easier. In Levy's novel, what strikes the reader is Hortense's painstaking and cultivated way of expressing herself through words and behaviour. She provides proof of her eloquence even in those private moments when she talks to herself:

> My two letters of recommendation each contained words that would open up the doors of any school to me. [...] my headmaster had seen fit to call my teaching skills proficient. [...] I was honoured to see he thought me expert. Miss Morgan, the formidable principle at my college declared me highly capable. And a highly capable expert I felt. This was the day I was going to present myself for a position as a teacher at the offices of education

authority and no pained-face, fool-fool man was going to imperil my elation. (448-49)

Despite all these qualifications, the "mother country" does not accept her for a teaching position, because she is from Jamaica. This shows the unfulfilled promise of language as a uniting thread of integration. In *The Nature of Blood*, the professed goal of establishing a society made of citizens with equal rights who share the same language, values and beliefs – *"The man at the hostel, he said to us, 'Welcome, my black brothers and sisters. You are helping us to understand what we are doing here.'"* (207-08) – in reality ends up producing a fragmented community in which the burden of learning and adapting falls entirely on the shoulders of the new arrivals and non-host nation education, culture and experience are devalued. Meanwhile, the white *élite*, relieved of its need to understand and confront views of the world that might challenge its own prejudices, carries on benefitting from the *status quo* undisturbed in its assumption of superiority. In the "promised land," Malka, after *"two years of intensive language study"* (200), attends a local university, majors in nursing, and yet remains unemployed. The only job she is seen fit to do is the one as a dancer at a men's club. All the expectations she had during her transfer to "Zion," where she and her people hoped to finally put an end to *"wandering [...] landless [and the] tilling of soil that did not belong to [them]"* (201), are superseded by disappointment soon after their arrival in Israel: *"The mayor of the town in which we were first placed complained. He had requested that he be sent only those who could sing and dance, so that he might form a folklore group for tourists"* (207). The Ethiopian black Jews soon discover they are regarded as an attraction for travellers who visit their home. They are not considered citizens with equal rights and are instead confined to living *"at the edge"* (207) of the Jewish community.

Through the character of Malka, Phillips also explores aspects of physical, social and mental space and the sort of exile Ethiopian black Jews are subjected to in the "promised land":

> Beyond the knowledge that she was presently an unemployed nurse, all he had managed to glean was that she was nearly thirty, and that she lived with her parents and younger sister at the edge of the city in one of the developments into which her people had been placed. [...] This was her first time in a hotel. When her family first arrived, they had been housed in what they were told was a hotel, but within a few weeks she came to understand that, in reality, the place was something called a hostel. And a hostel was most certainly not a hotel. [...] *Everywhere, we were told the same thing. First we will teach you the language, then when you leave the absorption centre you will be able to study at the university.* [...] *Have you seen the ugly housing at the edges of the city where we live?* [...] *Four of us, we live in one cramped apartment.* [...] *You say you rescued me. Gently plucked me from one century, helped me to cross two more, and then placed me in this time. Here. Now. But why?* (202-08; emphasis in the original)

Malka utters her feelings of exclusion and alienation for the first and only time when she dines with Stephan in a hotel: "'You do not want us here, do you?'" Stephan is civil in his answer, but the omniscient narrator voices his actual opinion a few lines later: "Dragging these people from their primitive world into this one [...] They belonged to another place" (210). In truth, the integration process seems to be, to paraphrase Phillips's words, a mere gesture of benevolence that quickly manifests its real purpose of exerting control on the new members of the community. A familiar historical pattern begins to take form: language functions less as a tool for cohesion and more as a means of enforcing subservience in newcomers. The new language slowly leads to the erosion of the minority language's status within the minority community itself, as well as of individual and cultural self-worth. Malka's parents are unable to fully adopt the new imposed customary manners and practices. They struggle to live their existences according to their Ethiopian traditions and culture. They resist the pressure to conform by secluding themselves. The only contact with the outside world is through television. From Malka's soliloquies emerges a picture of a broader community characterized by the lack of social cohesion between white and black Jews that extends to the family unit itself:

> [...] *And then, as we learnt the language and your ways, our parents felt as though they were losing us. It was hard for them. They were no longer responsible for their children.* [...] *My mother* [...] *finds it difficult to leave the apartment, for people stop and stare. And my father is incapable of adjusting to this land of clocks. I try to honour him as I would do in the old country, but it is impossible if he will not change.* [...] *My sister cries. Like my mother, she does not go out into the world.* [...] *Four of us, we live in one cramped apartment.* (207; emphasis in the original)

Phillips does not leave his readers entirely to themselves with the task of analyzing history from a kaleidoscopic perspective. In his essay "Blood" he writes about his novel:

> wherever one looks in European history, blood has been used as a pretext for the persecution of those whose faces do not fit on the canvas upon which the national portrait has been painted. [...] At first the writing appeared to be

flowing, if not freely, then at least purposefully towards a conclusion. (168-69)

Phillips (168) mentions "a final piece to the puzzle" which would allow him to relate the events of the past – not necessarily in chronological sequence or limited to specific locations. He at last discovers it in the story of the black Ethiopian Jewish community:

> And then one Bangkok morning I opened the "International Herald Tribune" and read the story of what had been occurring in Israel with the Ethiopian Jews [...] black Jews in Israel had been giving blood in the hope that it might be used to save somebody's life. However, the Israeli government, fearful of 'diseases' that might be contained in this blood, had instructed the medical teams to dump the 'black' blood. This 'secret' practice had now been exposed, and the black Jews were rioting and demanding that this racist policy be stopped. I could barely believe what I was reading. This, it turned out, was the story that would enable me to put the final piece of the narrative puzzle into place and finish my novel. (168)

For Phillips's reader, this missing piece provides a powerful new lens with which to look at history from a fresh perspective.

In 2016, Toni Morrison delivered a series of lectures on literature of belonging at Harvard University. In one of her speeches, she quotes Samuel Cartwright, a Southern physician and slaveholder who had made an impassioned plea for eugenics. Cartwright is the author of the 1851 "Report on the Diseases and Physical Peculiarities of the Negro Race," in which he develops a theory of his own of white superiority.

In his abstract reasoning, "according to unalterable physiological laws" Cartwright not only ascribes to "black blood" the cause and origin of African inferiority, but also identifies two illnesses which he defines as follows:

> "drapetomania", or the disease causing slaves to run away and "dysaesthesia aethiopica", a kind of mental lethargy that caused the negro 'to be like a person half asleep' (what slaveholders more commonly identified as "rascality"). [However] the forced exercise, so beneficial to the negro, is expended in cultivating [...] cotton, sugar, rice and tobacco, which, but for his labor [...] go uncultivated, and their products lost to the world. Both parties are benefitted – the negro as well as his master. (Qtd. in Morrison 4-5)

Morrison emphasizes the fact that Cartwright's self-serving logic, published in an authoritative journal, was common among slaveholders. Morrison (5) "wonders why, if these slaves were such a burden and threat, they were so eagerly bought, sold." She points out the slaveholders' opportunism, given that "It was probably universally clear – to sellers as well as the sold – that slavery was an inhuman, though profitable, condition" (6). And, this "profitable condition" goes in tandem with human being's conscious craving to exert control:

> for humans as an advanced species, our tendency to separate and judge those not in our clan as the enemy, as the vulnerable and the deficient needing control, has a long history not limited to the animal world or prehistoric man. Race has been a constant arbiter of difference, as have wealth, class and gender – each of which is about power and the necessity of control. (3)

Morrison's dismay at Cartwright's racial theories is echoed by Phillips's bewilderment at the newspaper article reporting the rejection of blood donated by blacks in the "promised land." Phillips devotes only roughly ten pages out of two hundred and twelve to Malka and the larger story of the black Ethiopian Jews. This small space within the narrative flow seems to mirror the little size of the piece of the puzzle he managed to find.

Despite his view of history as fragmented, Phillips identifies a recurring element in European history: a preoccupation with the vital fluid in the human body known as blood. Setting aside the biological function of blood, Phillips points out how this fluid, which is red in all vertebrates, functions as a marker of difference, authenticity and eligibility for the Western, white, European community. To him, *The Nature of Blood* is about

> Europe's obsession with homogeneity, and her inability to deal with the heterogeneity that is – in fact – her natural condition. The practice of using blood as a barometer of acceptability is very deeply ingrained in the European consciousness, and long before the present generation of non-white immigrants began to suffer because of this failure of European imagination, there were others – 'white', if you will – who had been identified as 'impure' and 'less' who suffered too. ("Blood" 168)

In *The Nature of Blood*, these others are those with Jewish roots in fifteenth-century Venice and the Jewish protagonists at the time of World War II.

Phillips encounters such "white others" in his adolescence. The young Phillips watches a programme on television on Nazism and the Holocaust:

> One thing I could not understand about the programme was why, when instructed to wear the yellow Star of David on their clothes, the Jews complied. They looked just

like any other white people to me, so who would know that they were different? As the programme progressed my sense of bemused fascination disappeared and was supplanted by my first mature feeling of outrage and fear. These yellow stars were marking them out for Bergen-Belsen and Auschwitz. I watched the library footage of the camps and realized both the enormity of the crime that was being perpetrated, and the precariousness of my own position in Europe. The many adolescent thoughts that worried my head can be reduced to one: 'If white people could do that to white people, then what the hell would they do to me?' ("Anne Frank's Amsterdam" 66-67)

Western education devotes a significant amount of time to teaching about the crimes against Jews and the ideology behind them; whereas European colonialism is only marginally discussed and any deeper analysis is relegated to specialized academic circles. In the seventies, in predominantly white British society the adolescent Phillips grows up acutely conscious of his own outsider experience and, unable to find narratives that spoke to his awareness of not fitting in, he turns to the closest parallel he can find: "the Jews were the only minority group discussed with reference to exploitation and racialism, and for that reason, I naturally identified with them" ("In the Ghetto" 53-54). Later on, the television series "World at War" has a powerful effect on Phillips's sensibility and triggers in him the desire to write:

> After that programme I wrote my first piece of fiction. A short story about a fifteen-year-old Jewish boy in Amsterdam who argues with his parents because he does not want to wear the yellow Star of David. […] My English literature teacher took this essay from me 'for publica-

tion', and that was the last I saw of it. ("Anne Frank's Amsterdam" 67)

It may be argued that *The Nature of Blood* represents a sequel to Phillips's "first piece of fiction" in which a Dutch adolescent manages to avoid deportation:

> Eventually there comes the knock on the door and his family are taken to the cattletrucks for 'resettlement'. En route the boy somehow manages to jump from the wagon, but in doing so he bangs his head. He lies bleeding by the railway embankment [...] the sunlight shining on his yellow star [...] attracts a kindly farmer's attention. The boy is taken to the farmhouse and saved. ("Anne Frank's Amsterdam" 67)

Eva in *The Nature of Blood*, by contrast, is discovered and sent to Bergen-Belsen. She comes to voice her mother's question, "How is it possible to be so angry with people who have done you no wrong?' (93), herself on the train to Bergen-Belsen (162). Although she physically survives the camp, she does not survive the psychological wounds of her internment and later commits suicide.

A plausible answer to Eva and her mother's question can be found in Freud's reflections on Judaism. On the whole, the main reason dwells in the Jews' assumption of being "the chosen people." Freud claims,

> I venture to assert that the jealousy which the Jews evoked in the other peoples by maintaining that they were the first-born, favourite child of God the Father has not yet been overcome by those others, just as if the latter had given credence to the assumption. Furthermore, among the customs through which the Jews marked off

their aloof position, that of circumcision made a disagreeable, uncanny impression on the others. The explanation is that it reminds them of the dreaded castration and of things in their primæval past which they would fain forget. Then there is lastly the most recent motive of the series. We must not forget that all the peoples who now excel in the practice of anti-Semitism became Christians only in relatively recent times, sometimes forced to it by bloody compulsion. One might say, they all are "badly christened"; under the thin veneer of Christianity they have remained what their ancestors were, barbarically polytheistic. They have not yet overcome their grudge against the new religion which was forced on them, and they have projected it on to the source from which Christianity came to them. The facts that the Gospels tell a story which is enacted among Jews, and in truth treats only of Jews, has facilitated such a projection. The hatred for Judaism is at bottom hatred for Christianity, and it is not surprising that in the German National-Socialist revolution this close connection of the two monotheistic religions finds such clear expression in the hostile treatment of both. (*Moses* 147-48)

Freud's choice of the words 'barbaric' and 'others' to refer non-Jews closely reflects Kapuściński's definition of the "Other" as an individual or group that is determined to be, in some identifiable way, unlike 'us' and is, consequently, attributed a superior/inferior (or civilized/primitive) character. As Phillips points out, "into the twentieth century, in the age of Marx, Freud and Einstein, the inferiority of the Jew was still a generally accepted European assumption" ("Anne Frank's Amsterdam" 69).

In his work on Judaism, Freud examines the figure of Moses in depth. If, with Freud (*Moses* 26), we assume that "Moses is an Egyptian – probably of noble origin – whom the myth undertakes to transform into a Jew," then in *The Nature of Blood* the character of Moshe gains a symbolic meaning.

The already quoted opening dialogue of *The Nature of Blood* involves a "boy of Romanian origin" (4) who questions Stephan about his future and the "promised land." We probably picture a mature Stephan, a kind of father figure, who tries to reassure a confused young man about the future by depicting a country that does not exist. The young man is aware that the "promised land" is not a gift that has been bestowed upon survivors but rather something that has to be attained and defended, through violence if necessary.

We can think of the boy with the highly charged name of Moshe as following in the footsteps of the biblical Moses by liberating Holocaust survivors under "British lock and key" (5) to lead them back home to the "promised land." Moshe's name suggests that he has to be seen against the role of a Moses of his people, a common epithet, bestowed on people such as Harriet Tubman, herself a former slave, who in her time came to be called the "Moses of her people" for her endeavours to lead other slaves from the southern states of the USA to freedom ("Harriet Tubman").

Sounding like an all-knowing, visionary authority figure, Stephan encourages Moshe to see himself as such a religious-political pioneer:

> The old world is dead. The survivors are here. Up there, gathered together on a hillside in Cyprus. The new world is just beginning, Moshe. And you are a part of it. [...] In Cyprus, I have watched as Europe spits the chewed bones in our direction. (The flesh she has already swallowed.) I have encouraged my young Moshe to think only of the future. Here is some money. Go. And remember, we will kill you if we ever see you again. Tell me, what will be the name of the country? [...] Moshe, think only of the future. My young friend Moshe. (9-12)

Phillips here draws attention to the extent to which a religion can paradoxically become a source of hate.

The Nature of Blood addresses the anger caused by the privilege denied to other monotheistic religions of being the "chosen people" as in this passage in which Eva describes her arrival in Bergen-Belsen:

> And now, at the end of the long platform, a uniformed man who possesses the gift of supreme confidence in himself. He waves first one way, and then the next, first this way, and then that, with no regard for affiliation. Destiny is a movement of his hand. Perhaps a quick question to make sure. Looks can deceive. How old? Healthy or ill? The old, pregnant, young, short, infirm. This way, please. Walk quickly. Roll up. Roll up. Already, a loudspeaker is blasting instructions to remove all clothing. Remove artificial limbs and eyeglasses. Tie your shoes together. Surrender any undeclared valuables and claim a receipt. Children go with the women. Where are we? The thin and the handicapped, this way, please. All gold rings, fountain pens, and chains. Roll up. Where is God? Where is your God? (162)

The mocking question suggests that for the Nazis the resentment toward Jewish people translates into a feeling of superiority and dominance. The same question follows Eva's memory of the entrance to the gas chamber:

> Hang your clothes neatly. Remember where. Put them on the hooks. Here is the towel. Here is the soap. Here is the towel. Here is the soap. Undress, please. You are going to heaven. Sanitary belts are ripped off. Blood everywhere. Shame. Shame. Now! These men without the

breeding to look away. Shower. For the lucky ones, no gas. Thank you, God. Uniforms. Barbed-wire everywhere. With electricity. Everywhere barbed-wire. Sky above. Where is God? Where is your God? (163)

Limited to orders, mocking and taunting the matter-of-fact language that Eva reports here underlines the mechanical, efficiency-driven approach to the extermination of Jews.

Eva's awareness of how much her life remains the same after the transfer from a Nazi concentration camp to a British displaced persons camp shows that the oppression of the Jewish people remains a historical constant, be it in pursuit of their extermination or to preserve colonial and later postcolonial economic interests in the Middle East.

* * *

When Eva concludes her account of her last day in Cyprus – "Tomorrow, they will release me into an empty world with only Gerry for company" (48) – the omniscient narrator catapults readers across time and space. But despite the five-century gap, readers are now confronted with yet another form of oppression:

> The Jews had first begun journeying to Portobuffole in 1424, many of them migrating from Colonia in Germany. Back in 1349, the Christian people of that region had suddenly become incensed and irrational from fear of the plague, and the Jews began to suffer as this Christian hysteria manifested itself in violence. [...] In 1424, the Jews of Colonia were finally expelled for good, and most decided to travel to the Republic of Venice, where it was rumoured that life was more secure. (50-51)

2 The Jewish Question 113

During the Middle Ages and the Renaissance, the Republic of Venice was a leading trading and maritime power. It is in this context that the omniscient narrator's voice brings up a delicate, diplomatic concern for the Republic: "The Most Serene Republic of Venice had recently made a reluctant peace with the infidel Turk and, once again, the Venetian army was being demobilized" (48). This military detail may appear superfluous, but falls in place when the quasi-Othello's voice takes over. At this juncture, "the Republic of Venice" functions as a transition from the issue of prejudice based on religious beliefs to the issue of skin complexion (cf. 3.1, 3.2).

Definitions of terms relevant to the novel are interpolated in the narrative. They resemble encyclopaedic entries supplemented with the personal view of the author on the subject:[6]

> GHETTO: It is generally thought that the word *ghetto* was first used to describe the section of Venice where, in the sixteenth century, Jews were ordered to live apart from Christians in a 'marshy and unwholesome site' to the north of St Mark's. The Italian word *ghetto* means 'iron foundry', the Venetian Jews being forced to live next to the site of a former foundry. Ghettos are generally subject to serious overpopulation, and they exercise a debilitating effect on the self-confidence of their inhabitants. (160; emphasis in the original)

Ghettos do not only affect the individual's self-confidence; they also limit their access to economic and cultural participation in the society at large.

Bassi and di Lenardo (5) comment on the Venetian Ghetto[7] that it

---

[6] Other interpolations can be found in the epigraph to section 2.1.2.3 as well as in the section devoted to the quasi-Othello.
[7] The first establishment of the Ghetto in history occurred in Venice in 1516 (6).

prompted a large number of Jews from the mainland to seek sanctuary in the city. It was to be an inclusive/exclusive area for a nucleus of cosmopolitan Jews, with a view to guaranteeing the continuance of their essential commercial services in exchange for a degree of protection atypical of a Europe ever prone to outbreaks of anti-Semitic persecution.

Bassi and di Lenardo (9) puncture any notion on the part of the reader that altruism may have played a role in Venice's offer to take in fleeing Jews – the city understood that Jews provided "essential economic services" and contributed significantly to the wealth of the Republic:

> The area was not only peripheral but also without urban appeal, lacking in significant architecture, isolated and hemmed in by canals; it boasted a monotonous uniformity, both in type and quality (poor) of building. [...] The obligation for Jews to reside in the Ghetto had its effect on the outward aspect of the space, the only place to build was upwards. (Bassi and di Lenardo 10)

The creation of a highly regulated, carefully planned and deliberately separated quarter assigned to a minority group recalls Toni Morrison's reflections on the human craving to exert control over the "Other." In this Venetian context, it manifests itself through the control "of day to day activities, the observance of rules of hygiene in accordance with civic usage, the protection, regulation and location of [religious] rites" (Bassi and di Lenardo 9).

In the novel we are confronted with yet another form of domination of Jews. As the omniscient narrator points out, the Jews in Portobuffole "arrived as foreigners, and foreigners they remained":

> Although the Venetian *Grand Council* sought to discourage the propagation of false ideas about the Jews (for these people were an important part of the republic's economy), the doge's inner *Council of Ten* nevertheless passed a law according to which the Jews were instructed to distinguish themselves by yellow stitching on their clothes. People detested the Jews for a variety of reasons, but the most often cited referred to their position in society as people who would loan money at an interest, more often than not requiring extravagant security from the borrower. [...] By obliging the Jews to lend money in exchange for permission to live in their territory, the Republic of Venice could pretend to be implementing a policy of some tolerance towards the Jews, while serving its own interests and ignoring the fact that it was further exposing the Jews to the multiple dangers of Christian hostility. (51-53)

This prescription of identifying stitching along with the establishment of the ghetto ensured that the "Other" remain both physically and culturally different.

The omniscient narrator attributes the hostility against the Jews to Christian misinterpretation of Jewish spiritual practices:

> Not only had the Jews killed Jesus Christ, but during Holy Week it was common practice for them to re-enact this crime and kill a Christian child in order that they might draw out the fresh blood and knead some of it into the unleavened bread which they ate during their own Easter celebration, known as Passover. (51-52)

Similarly later in time, Portobuffole becomes another breeding ground for the aforementioned biased opinion of Jews as primitive and barbaric:

> Whereas the state reluctantly admitted their need for the Jews, the church required no such diplomacy. The Franciscans, in particular, preached vehemently against the Jews [...] Jews, who were little more than merchants of tears and drinkers of human blood. (55-56)

The Doge's initial apprehension of "the propagation of false ideas about the Jews" materializes after Easter . Suddenly, rumours emerge that a foreign boy is missing and that Jews have kidnapped him: "The Jews had killed an innocent Christian boy named Sebastian New. They had dared to make a sacrifice in the Christian town of Portobuffole" (59).

Eventually, rumours are taken seriously, and in order to establish the truth of this particular story, the Doge comes to the conclusion that the accuracy of the evidence can be verified by judicial cross-examination. For this reason, a number of suspects are taken into custody and questioned. The procedure is a cruel exercise in validating unfounded hearsay and bigotry. In the omniscient narrator's meticulous description of events we learn about torture of witnesses and the Venetian justice system that resorts to this means of coercion.

Owing to the controversial nature of the case which is diplomatically difficult to handle, the three indicted Jews go to two trials. In Portobuffole the verdict cannot be reached. Eventually, in Venice, the defendants are found guilty and sentenced to death.

Before the execution, Servadio, one of the Jewish prisoners

> begged his companions not to drink, despite the fact that they were tormented by thirst. Although he did not tell them, he was also thinking that their bodies would burn

more easily if they were dried up, thereby reducing their suffering and maintaining a more dignified image. (152)

This image of burning bodies foreshadows the emergence of the crematoriums and the Nazi goal of rendering mass death as efficient as any finely tuned industrial process. The omniscient narrator at one point describes the brutal Nazi death camps, and how Jews were forced, on threat of their own deaths, to aid with the disposal of gas chamber victims. Like Servadio in the above passage, Eva, the member of a *Sonderkommando* considers the desirability of a quick termination of life from the victim's perspective: "Clothed bodies burn slowly. Decayed bodies burn slowly. In her mind she cries, fresh and naked, please. Women and children burn faster than men. Fresh naked children burn the fastest" (170).

The omniscient narrator materializes unobtrusively in key moments as a means to fill a gap in the narrative. Its role is fundamental in providing facts and feelings from an external perspective. This, in turn, is able to offer objective, detailed, accurate descriptions of circumstances, methods or procedures such as the scientific description of the gassing employed by Nazis (cf. 2.1.2.2).

In sixteenth century Venetian society, the Jews as the "Other" are not given the opportunity to express themselves other than through this narrator. However, before the execution Servadio's own voice takes over and offers his side of the story:

> We rise with the sun. I turn from Giacobbe to Moses, then back to Giacobbe. My brothers, do not let them see you weeping like this. Today, we must leave this cell and begin our final journey, but let us do so with dignity. There will be no tears and no pleading. We will maintain our fast and continue to refuse to drink water. We are going home. [...] The journey to the north by water, and then back here to St Mark's on foot, is designed to hu-

miliate us. But they are not our masters. We must obey only God. [...] (*I tell you, I have never heard of this boy, Sebastian New. I have never seen such a boy. I know not what you are talking about. My wife is suffering, my family is drowning in tears. Why? Who is this Sebastian New? What are you talking about?)* [...] To these men's ears, my words are stale. Giacobbe and Moses continue to weep. [...] I am thirsty, but I will not drink water. We must refuse to drink water. (181-182; emphasis in the original)

This section aims to illustrate the multiple facets of "Otherness" that are scattered across the complex narrative of *The Nature of Blood*. Reading the novel may be compared to wandering through history, and Phillips seems to guide his readers by allowing them to explore a kaleidoscopic image of history. This mental optical instrument is able to produce symmetrical patterns of events whose similarities lead to a multidirectional understanding of historical facts inaccurately believed to be unrelated to each other. Rothberg's (164) statement on the novel epitomizes what I perceive to be the main purpose of Phillips's work: "*The Nature of Blood* testifies to the existence of new possibilities for thinking the relatedness of the unrelatable."

3 Fragmented History

3.1 The Disputable Concept of Race

> "The fact is, I was more interested in writing about the human heart than I was in addressing 'issues' – black or otherwise. [...] I was keen that at [my work's] centre there would be the human heart. And, as we all discovered in the late sixties when the first heart transplant operation took place in South Africa, the human heart has no color."
> – Caryl Phillips ("Necessary Journeys" 126)

Robert J. C. Young's introduction to his study of postcolonialism is a useful place to start to gain insight into the sources of racial prejudice:

> Colonial and imperial rule was legitimized by anthropological theories which increasingly portrayed the peoples of the colonized world as inferior, childlike, or feminine, incapable of looking after themselves (despite having done so perfectly well for millennia) and requiring the paternal rule of the west for their own best interests. [...] The basis of such anthropological theories was the concept of race. In simple terms, the west-non-west relation was thought of in terms of whites versus the non-white races. (*Postcolonialism* 2)

The belief in a twofold humankind started to take root in the fifteenth century, in the wake of the first European conquests overseas. The subsequent encounter with people who were not only visibly different but also had different ways of living required a word that could express these forms of diversity. At that time, the word 'race' did not have a single, uniform meaning. Ivan Hannaford (5) lists European words with heterogeneous etymologies that were pressed into service to categorize visibly different human beings.

The word 'race' entered Western languages late, coming into general use in Northern Europe at about the middle of the sixteenth century. "There is no word bearing a resemblance to it in Hebrew, Greek, or Roman literature" (Hannaford 3-6). Early denotations are unrelated to the later meaning attached to it.

It was only in the late seventeenth century that 'race' began to connotate the idea that the human species is partitioned on the basis of physical and genetic traits. Europeans went on to hold that superficial distinguishing features were responsible for differences in culture, development and civilization that differentiate one community from another (Hannaford 6-10).

In a similar manner, Bassi ("Oltre la 'razza'" 108) states that "'race' is an arbitrary category" (translation mine).[1] He points out that even though the term is now most often associated with physical traits such as skin colour, blood (in the sense of lineage), or skull shape and size, the word has historically been associated with a variety of meanings. The common denominator in every case, however, is the use of race as a signifier of the 'Other' (108-09).

Even before the word 'race' came in use to group people on the basis of their skin colour, European societies were already organized into a hierarchical class system based on social rank. European nations were composed of peoples from different regions, and, as Banton and Hardwood (19) remind us, "sometimes the lines of political tension coincided with those of origin, so that evidence about different customs of the original groups could be used in political [and/or religious] argument."

In the fifteenth century, European settlements were composed of such large numbers of diverse peoples that the existing structures of organizations – local kings, priests, tribal leaders, heads of households

---

[1] "[L]a 'razza' [è] una categoria arbitraria" ("Oltre la 'razza'"108).

– began to feel inadequate. In addition, scientific and technological development became a further key factor in European transformations. The ensuing major societal, political and economic changes triggered the voyages of exploration and trade, and determined "what it was the travellers went in search of and even to some extent what they saw" (Banton and Harwood 14).

The discovery of peoples in the New World and the challenge of establishing a relationship with them prepared the ground for disparities. On those first encounters with the "Other," overseas populations were regarded as primitive when measured by European standards. Upon their arrival in what they blithely decided to call the New World, Europeans were confronted with realities that somehow reflected their primitive past, a reminder they were inclined to deliberately erase from their minds. Over and above different ways of life,

> there was [also] a basic idea, grounded in European thought, that black was the colour of sin and death. […] From early times European Christianity took over and utilised this association between blackness and evil, so that in medieval romances the enemies of the knights are commonly said to be black; in the earliest illuminated manuscripts the tormentors of Christ are painted with black faces; […] little wonder, then, that when Europeans first met black people, their minds were full of these prior associations. (Banton and Harwood 14-15)

Later, such suppositions gave way to a new perception of the "Other" as "innocent and uncorrupted" (16) people who persisted in maintaining their societies at a primitive stage. This interpretation of cultures and peoples they knew very little about legitimized Western feelings of superiority, which replicated the familiar, highly stratified social divisions prevalent within Western societies.

The first encounters with people outside their known world gave rise to a question to which European intellectuals were unable to provide a plausible answer, namely that of the survival of barbarism. The explanation that evolved over time sought to reconcile the apparent lack of consistency in human development with the divine design belief that underpinned Western thought at the time. The conclusion was that (a) the degree of advancement of societies was due to moral causes, i.e. culture, and that (b) those moral causes were rooted in physical differences in human anatomy (Banton and Harwood 17).

The awareness of the existence of non-European realities stimulated the development of theories that could justify this form of diversity, even if, at least at the beginning, the focus was on the norms and structures that governed individual societies. One of the earliest sociologists, Adam Ferguson offered another perspective on the matter. He stated that the individual is a social being, and the societal welfare depends on the individual's ability to progress. Ferguson chiefly differentiated human groupings into three categories:

> savage, barbarous and polished – defining each category in terms of characteristic economic activities, patterns of social subordination and constellations of opinions. He thought the clue to progress lay in man's success in developing the social organisation appropriate to his environment. (Banton and Harwood 17)

Although Ferguson attempted to explain differences using an ethnological approach, he did not go so far as to contradict the view of biblical scholars who insisted that, according to scripture, "all men were the descendants of an original pair and were of the same nature" (18). It follows from this that the above-mentioned categorization of societal groups cannot be justified by scripture.

In the historical context of the early modern and the modern age religious proclamations that all men shared "the same nature," began to sound doubtful and anachronistic. Christians attempted to follow the rational lead which gave rise to two schools of thought: "the monogenists," who believed in a single origin, as provided in the Bible, and "the polygenists," who, while complying with religious teachings, believed in adapting scripture to the changing circumstances. It was the latter group who broke with the orthodox view of equality between all men and stated that "different races or tribes had been separately created" (Banton and Harwood 18). The evidence for this assertion was never very solid: "Those who defended the [slave] trade did not want the support of doctrines that conflicted with the Bible" (Banton and Harwood 18-19).

In such a flurry of intellectual activities, prejudice against non-Western, non-white people was increasing in the "civilized world." If religion proved to be unable to explain the existence of a variety of human beings, the pragmatic approach was equally inadequate. For instance, many naturalists saw both vegetable and animal life as a continuum, a great chain of organisms. In this hypothetical chain the structure was so compact to the point of being difficult to single out "which stood on either side as links in the chain. It was easy to accommodate to this theory newly emerging ideas of racial inferiority, for blacks could be regarded as links in the chain intermediate between white men and orangutans" (18).

As a matter of course, the emerging ideas of racial inferiority gave way to further attempts to explain stages of social development in racial terms. Banton and Harwood draw attention to a highly controversial work circulating at that time written by the Jamaican-born British colonial administrator, Edward Long. His *History of Jamaica* (1774) proved to be a justification of slavery and exploitation of Africans who were perceived as animals. According to Long,

> blacks and whites were different species; that hybrids between the two were eventually infertile; that blacks were closer to the apes. Africans, in his opinion, were 'brut-

ish', ignorant, idle, crafty, treacherous, bloody, thievish, mistrustful and superstitious people.' They had on their heads not hair but wool. They were inferior mentally and gave off a bestial smell. Their physical nature was fundamentally different from that of Europeans. (Banton and Harwood 19)

Such theories, like Samuel Cartwright's and those dealt with by Toni Morrison, served to provide a superficial veneer of scientific fact and respectability to racism proved especially useful in excusing and justifying the Western, colonial economy based on forced labour and the illegal takeover of resources.

Like Banton and Harwood, Paul Gilroy shed light on religion as "the older understanding of alterity [that] was based primarily upon categories of faith and religious practice as indexes of cultural distance" ("Suffering" 31). The subsequent separation of religion from intellectual thought coincided with the period when Europeans commenced their overseas territorial expansion. The discovery of new lands for political prestige and economic gain was accompanied – and aided – by the growth of technical innovations, rational thinking and the scientific method. This blossoming of secular intellectual thought also brought with it dubious theories such as the hierarchical categorization of the human species by skin complexion. These ideas, which promoted a view of humans arranged into successive ranks with each level subordinate to the one above, legitimized "the polarized opposition of black to white" (31) only to perpetuate slavery.

The physical traits that distinguish ethnic groups from one another do not generate superior/inferior individuals. The visible differences merely represent a result of geographic and environmental conditions. The concept of race was created as a convenient tool for identifying populations (rather than evaluating the degree of their humanity). In 1953, on the occasion of the Seventh Session of the General Conference of Unesco, Harold Cyril Bibby (7) reminded his audience that there is absolutely no biological evidence to support the racial superiority of one human race over any other human race. His text aimed at helping teachers to strive against prejudices that are likely to be acquired during childhood:

> There is no biological warrant at all for such terms as 'the Aryan race', 'the British race', 'the Jewish race', 'the Arab race' and so on. 'Aryan' is a linguistic term for a hypothetical early language, 'British' is a political term for a particular group of nations sharing certain historical traditions and constitutional forms, 'Jewish' is a socio-theological term for people with an ancient religious tradition and with recognizable customs, 'Arab' is an ecological term for those who lead or have comparatively recently led a particular type of seminomadic life in the Middle-East. None of these are 'races' in any proper biological sense: indeed, to speak of an 'Aryan race' is as great an abuse of words as to speak of a 'black-skinned language', and this should be made clear to children.

Bibby hoped to prevent future instances of intolerance, prejudice, discrimination, cruelty, exploitation and mass-murder through education. The concept of race is complex and extends itself to the fields of biology, psychology, sociology, anthropology, geography and history. By reason of this, he strongly encouraged teachers to guide children to the proper use of language along with cultivating autonomous and critical thinking (8-10). Given that the origin of racial prejudice has many and confused roots, Bibby addressed his text more specifically to the areas of governments in charge of education, especially in countries with a colonial past. Geography and history books had, according to Bibby, a responsibility to provide a more inclusive view of history, one which included the history of the colonized peoples (54). However, as postcolonial literature demonstrates, this pedagogic project is still struggling to find its rightful place in school curricula.[2]

* * *

In *The Nature of Blood*, Phillips eloquently brings up the similarities between African and Jewish historical patterns. For instance, the origin of prejudice against both groups has roots in Christianity as has been pointed out above in the context of black as the colour of sin and death. Consequently, it is hardly surprising that the first encounter with Africans could only arouse feelings of fear and estrangement. For Judaism, Phillips argues thus:

> Jews became the victims of theft, repression, extermination and exile, and as Christianity spread so did anti-Semitic feeling. In Christian eyes the Jews were always going to have to atone for the death of Christ. [...] Theories were propagated, all of them supposedly serious, to try and justify Jewish inferiority. They included the 'fact' that Jews were going to take over the world, that Jews have bigger backsides, differently sized and shaped skulls, bigger noses, a greater propensity towards crime, and do not like to mix. Four decades into the twentieth century, in the age of Marx, Freud and Einstein, the inferiority of the Jew was still a generally accepted European assumption. ("Anne Frank's Amsterdam" 68-69)

This mirrors appearance-fixated evidence that underpinned theories developed to justify African inferiority. Charles Hamilton Smith's *The Natural History of the Human Species* (1848) is emblematic of this

---

[2] Cf. 2.2, where I mention Ngũgĩ wa Thiong'o and his school experience at the élite English school that aimed at turning out "civic-minded blacks who would work within the parameters of the existing racial state."

type of race-focused pseudo-scientific work. Smith asserted that there had always been three distinct human types which were classified in the following sequence: the Caucasian, the Mongolian, and, lowest of all, the Negro. Smith claimed "the Negro's lowly place in the human order was a consequence of the small volume of his brain" (Banton and Harwood 28). Similarly, theories that associate inferiority with reprehensible behaviours, such as the Jews' "greater propensity towards crime," are in evidence in the four-volume *Essay on the Inequality of Human Races* (1854) by Count Joseph Arthur de Gobineau. Gobineau maintained Smith's division of human beings into three categories – "white," "yellow" and "black" – and stated that "the physical differences produce radical dissimilarity and inequality, which extend to the moral life" (Hughes 205). According to Gobineau, human beings had passed through a series of stages in the course of which the three major races had become separated. This established the superiority of the white people. Consequently, Gobineau strongly discouraged race-mixing, which he perceived as a deterioration of humanity. Centuries later, his assertions were used by German national socialism to proclaim the superiority of the Aryan "race" above other ethnic groups (Banton and Harwood 29-30).

In 1859, Charles Darwin asserted in his *On the Origin of Species* that all species of life have descended from common ancestors. According to his scientific theories of evolution and natural selection the changes in the characteristics of a population of animals or plants occur over successive generations. Such gradual transformations in anatomy, biology, anthropology, ethnology and philology "act together in a series of co-terminous natural events, thus enabling for the first time an idea of evolving 'self-determining' races to emerge" (Hannaford 273). So great was the impact of Darwin's idea on the nineteenth century that scholars in the social sciences soon began viewing politics, economics and human societies as resembling living organisms governed by the principle of natural selection and evolution (Hannaford 273-74).

It is not surprising, given Europe's fascination with the concept of race, that Darwin's theory would (with some tweaking to fit racist agendas) resonate with intellectuals at the time. As is obvious from reading Hannaford, the topic was already a subject of interest at least two centuries before Darwin published *On the Origin of Species*, including writers such as Hobbes, Herder, Comte and Marx.

It is often believed that racial prejudice started with the discovery of the Americas. However, when we consider the use of the word 'race' before the rise of European colonialism, it becomes clear that in some European cultures – specifically, Spanish, Portuguese and Italian where race was connected to lineage – race had long been associated with perceived notions of superiority of one group over the other. In those countries, prejudice was directed at members of the community who occupied the lower rungs in the social ladder. When Europeans arrived in the New World they simply recycled their ideas of class and applied them to race complete with all the superior/inferior prejudices of the European class system. Arguably, the three pillars of oppression (class, gender and race) can be found in nearly all cultures. The European innovation lies in the fact that they took their bigotry on tour when they decided the rest of the planet was theirs to colonize.

In trying to understand the widespread phenomenon of race-based oppression, the significant role played by language over the centuries cannot be overlooked. Stuart Hall acknowledges that race is made up of intricate parts or aspects that are difficult to analyze and suggests an alternative investigation. To the Marxist sociologist, race does not imply an idea or an abstract concept, race is rather a conversational practice. Hall sees race as a discourse that gives rise to different denotations that are strictly connected to the historical period in which they are employed (Mellino 12). Through this lens of conversational practice, Hall identifies two dominant tendencies: economic and sociological. The economic aspect is related to societal disparities based on skin colour. These disparities are understood as a consequence of the economic structures and processes that belong to societies. The sociological facet focuses on the relationships among different ethnic groups and subsequent forms of domination or political subordination based on the exploitation of racial differences (Hall, "Race" 68-69).

* * *

Hatred of a specific social or ethnic group holds a major place in human dynamics. Hatred as the urge to ostracize and possibly eliminate that which appears alien, functions as a binding force enabling social groups to define themselves in comparison to others. The perception of those outside of their group in a collectively threatening and unfavourable light allows a specific group to gain a self-definition and a sense of identity. It is an identity and definition based on negation, i.e. I am not what I hate. Prejudices differ in their content. In the context of anti-Semitism, the particular characteristics attributed to the target group cover a whole range of stereotypes such as the Jew as a greedy person capitalist; or the Jew as an intellectual who seeks to disrupt the existing order and endangers society (Riesigl and Vodak 57-68).

Sander L. Gilman and Steven Theodore Katz (33-34) underscore the roots of anti-Semitism in Christian theology. According to this conception, Jews carried out the work of Satan, striving to undermine Christianity and the promise of salvation brought by the church. In *The Nature of Blood*, this type of Christian anti-Semitism is found in the detailed account of "The Venetian trial against the Jews of Portobuffole" (149): "Considering that this case with the Jews is full of evil and goes against the honour of Jesus Christ, it is necessary to draw some conclusions with the maximum amount of application (105)." And later we read: "The state prosecutor concluded with the assertion that surely it was the devil himself who gave these people the idea to kill innocent Christian children, and now they must die" (150).

Although the Jewish new arrivals did not constantly have to live in fear for their safety as they had in Colonia, their integration into Venetian society never materialized:

> Initially, the people of the republic accepted the Jews from Colonia with all the mistrust that is common among people who do not know one another. Sadly, as the years passed, this mistrust did not abate. [The Jews] chose not to eat or drink with the Christians, and they refused to attend to their heavy German accents. They looked different. [...] The Jews ate neither pork nor red meat sold from a butcher, preferring instead to slaughter live animals and then drain the blood. [...] eight days after a son was born they had huge celebrations in honour of the boy's circumcision. Those who glimpsed the Jewish men praying claimed that they covered their whole bodies, including their heads, with a large shawl that made them appear both animal-like and foolish. These Jews arrived as foreigners, and foreigners they remained. (51)

The Jews were clearly viewed with a mixture of contempt and fear, but, as mentioned earlier, they were also valued for the unsavoury services they provided and the money they contributed to the city coffers. The wealth they brought with them, more than humanitarian concerns, was the principal reason the republic opened its doors to the refugees from the north. If the Jews were seen as contributing much needed "large-scale capital investment" (53) to an economically weakened Venice, their contribution to social and public life remained marginal.

Ashley Dawson (87) identifies one of the omniscient narrators of the Venetian section of the novel as "Andrea Dolfin, an aristocrat appointed by the Venetian republic to rule Portobuffole." For Dawson, the leader of Portobuffole embodies the convergence of political and religious currents that sustained Venetian prejudice towards the Jewish community. He argues that Dolfin, thanks to his privileged political and social standing within the republic, is in a unique insider position to provide an exhaustive depiction of the judicial examination of the death of a Christian boy (59).

The Venetian aristocrats' ambivalence towards the Jewish religious minority in their city replicates itself centuries later in a wider European context. This juxtaposition of different time periods creates a historical mirroring effect that reveals that religious differences may, in part, help explain the long standing estrangement between Christian and Jewish communities in Europe, but the fires of anti-Jewish sentiments were also fuelled by other, much more worldly concerns. In *The Origins of Totalitarianism*, Hannah Arendt makes it possible to draw a parallel between the events in fifteenth-century Venice and Nazi Germany when she argues that, in the early twentieth century, class tension and fear of Jewish political advancement contributed significantly to anti-Semitism:

> Many […] bankers were Jews and, even more important, the general figure of the banker bore definite Jewish traits for historical reasons. Thus the leftist movement of the lower middle class and the entire propaganda against banking capital turned more or less anti-Semitic, a development of little importance in industrial Germany but of great significance in France and, to a lesser extent, in Austria. For a while it looked as though the Jews had indeed for the first time to come into direct conflict with another class without interference from the state. […] The position of the Jews as bankers depended not upon loans to small people in distress, but primarily on the issuance of state loans. […] The social resentment of the lower middle classes against the Jews turned into a highly explosive political element, because these bitterly hat-

ed Jews were thought to be well on their way to political power. (*Origins* 37)

The behaviour of a large number of European countries has been characterized by a penchant for expanding political authority and prestige beyond their own borders. This intention to extend power to distant lands requires, in Phillips's words quoted above, substantial "large-scale capital investment" that, more often than not, leads to societal disparities. From the sixteenth to the early nineteenth century the economy of the British Empire, for instance, largely depended on commodity crops, goods and clothing produced in the New World by African slave labour. The exploitation of people regarded as inferior is one striking similarity in European dealings with both African and Jewish peoples. For example, one component of the carefully planned Nazi genocide of "inferior races," which targeted, but was not limited to, Jews, was the use of detainees as forced labour in the concentration camps. The Jews were deported from the ghettos in sealed freight trains to extermination camps where survivors of the journey, prior to being killed in gas chambers, were put to work as slaves often in the service of large German industrial groups.

In *The Nature of Blood* this chapter of history is illustrated by Eva's account. Imprisoned Jews, who quickly realized the meaning and purpose of those camps surrounded by barbed wires, desperately sought ways to postpone their death: "Hungry. Angry. Pathetic people clinging meekly to the remnants of their lives and wondering if, through hard work, they might earn the right to live" (162). The task of a *Sonderkommando* member like Eva was one way, however temporary, that detainees sought to prolong their lives, even if, in practical terms, it did not provide any respite from any of the other daily hardships of the camp. Anti-Semitism is so ingrained in the culture, so internalized by both victims and perpetrators, that even in this brutally pared down, animal-like struggle to survive, Eva manages to exhibit feelings of prejudice towards other fellow Jews whom she describes as "dirty, uncultivated people from the east" (169).

In 1999, twelve years after the first edition of *The European Tribe*, in which Phillips chronicles his journey through the multi-ethnic Europe of the nineteen-eighties, the author added further updated reflections in the "Afterword to the Vintage Edition." These reflections equally hold for *The Nature of Blood*:

> I suppose the point that I am trying to make is a straightforward one. Europeans are human beings. They are subject to the same insecurities, the same inability to forgive, the same prejudices, the same disturbing nationalism, the same cruelties, as any other people. Europe's global pre-eminence has disappeared during the second half of the twentieth century [...] Europeans squabble, they fight, they kill because of tribal affiliations. They relish the opportunity of a new flag, or a new national anthem, as much as anybody else. Like all people, in order to assert and affirm who they are, they are quick to identify who they are not. Of course, this often means identifying differences in other people that they decide are impossible for them to tolerate.
>
> The people who are the most easily identifiable as the 'other' are those of a different race, or religion, or both. Europeans continue to persecute such people, and the evidence of this racism is so overwhelming that it serves little purpose to repeat the litany of headlines or recall the countless episodes of injustice. (132)

Even though in this passage Phillips resorts to the word 'race,' in his novels, this arbitrary category is never employed by his narrating voices. For instance in *The Nature of Blood*, the quasi-Othello, who arrives in Venice from a foreign land constantly emphasizes his status as outsider within the Venetian community without using that word:

> I had made no friends among these people, and my standing in society rested solely upon my reputation in the field. My reputation. It was to be hoped that this one small word might lay to rest any hostility that my natural appearance might provoke. My reputation. Some among these people, both high and low, were teaching me to think of myself as a man less worthy than the person I knew myself to be. My own people, although degraded and without the sophistication and manners of these Venetians, at least regarded me with respect and dignity, and among them I had many friends, and some few enemies, all of whom were easily identifiable. Among the Venetians, all was confusion as I attempted to distinguish those who beheld my person with scorn and contempt, from those who simply looked upon me with the curiosity that one would associate with a child. (118)

Ironically, "the sophistication and manners" Venetians liked to affect more aptly characterize the "man born of royal blood, a mighty warrior," who was "summoned [...] to stand at the very centre of the empire" (107). From the African General's point of view, it is "his own people" who are honest and well-mannered, not the worldly, civilized Venetians.

In the next section I will discuss in greater detail the quasi-Othello, whose narrative eloquently illustrates the stereotypical tropes used to define the "Other."

Theories of racial inequality were produced because imperialism and capitalists needed an ideological justification for exploiting dark-sinned people overseas. The Christian belief that all humans are equally created in God's image gave way to a very gradual process where little by little exceptions were introduced and gained acceptance because they fit nicely with economic interests, as was the case with Jews. As Phillips's characters manifest, the term race is a linguistic weapon employed by the so-called civilized world of the West to oppress minorities anytime white supremacy is in question.

3.2 The Quasi-Othello

> Neutral is white. The default is white [...] the whole of humanity is coded as white. Blackness, however, is considered the 'other' and therefore to be suspected. Those who are coded as a threat in our collective representation of humanity are not white.
> – Reni Eddo-Lodge (85)

In *The Nature of Blood*, Malka and the quasi-Othello draw attention to what Phillips ("European Tribe" 121) calls Europe's "lack of a cogent sense of history." Their stories defy the narrow roles traditionally assigned to Africans in European history books:

> It is no coincidence that at the great European schools of learning, history is still the most respected of degrees. But history is also the prison from which Europeans often speak, and in which they would confine black people. It is a false history, an unquestioning and totally selfish one, in which whites civilize and discover and the height of sophistication is to sit in a castle with a robe of velvet and a crown dispensing order and justice. (121)

The Nature of Blood attempts to restore the threads missing from the incomplete tapestry of European history.

Instead of staying with Eva as she travels from Cyprus to London, readers are catapulted into another age of prejudice towards Jews, late mediaeval Western Europe at the time after the plague. Readers find themselves yet again in a world recently liberated from existential danger paralleling, in many ways, the end of the Second World War and the closing of the death camps. As in the post-war reality of Eva's story, in Portobuffole old scars and the self-protective reflexes of the survivors are still very much inescapable features of day to day life and the figure of the stranger triggers suspicion towards the Jews fleeing from Germany. Three innocent Jews are subjected not to one but two trials before they are sentenced to death. At this point in the novel, a new narrating voice irrupts and momentarily diverts readers' attention from the trial. They receive a sudden, cryptic description of "the most un-Venetian of women [who] sleeps peacefully, her dark hair a gown about her neck and shoulders" (106) along with some additional hints about this mysterious character: "I am familiar with the renowned deceit of the Venetian courtesan, yet I have taken a Venetian for a wife. Has some plot been hatched about me? I am a foreigner" (106).

The word 'foreigner' as well as other terms related to its semantic field is used as a character's calling card. Phillips's narrators usually use the word as soon as they join the narration. This new narrating voice belongs to an outcast struggling with the antithetical feelings of belonging-longing, inclusion-exclusion, superior-inferior. Ledent refers to him as the Othello-like character: the figure of "a man born of royal blood, [...] who, at one time, could view himself only as a poor slave, [and now] stand[s] at the very centre of the empire" (107).

It takes this character over one hundred pages to make its first appearance. His introduction in exactly the middle of novel (on page 106 of 212 pages) is not accidental. Similarly to Stephan's case, we can read this quasi-Othello as a hub representing a point of convergence from which connections among heterogeneous historical events radiate. This is corroborated by the unfolding of storylines that depart from the character's account of events related to his stay in Venice. Later, readers are dragged into a twist of narrations that are "counterpointed with a complex network of correspondences" (Ledent 136). They are soon after confronted with the deportation of Jews to concentration camps, a pattern of forced labour recalling aspects of the Atlantic slave trade. From the camps, readers then move forward in time to reach Eva on the train headed to London. Londoners' attitudes towards a newcomer like her are a carbon copy version of Londoners' attitudes toward the Windrush generation, who began to arrive in the mother country in 1948 (cf. 2.1.2.3) and, to a certain degree, Venetians' attitudes towards the quasi-Othello. Lastly, Malka portrays her transfer to Israel – an instance of uprooting an African people with echoes of the shipment of Africans to the New World centuries earlier – and the flaws in the ambitious project known as the promised land. Phillips groups narratives around a central theme/character instead of straining to put together a unified story, leaving the act of unifying the different strands to the reader.

Similarly, to his co-participants in the narrative, the dark-skinned character disseminates information about himself without arranging it in sequence. Immediately after introducing himself as a "foreigner" (106), he discusses his marital status and presents his "new wife." He then goes on to reveal his double status as outsider from a strange land and respected General in the Venetian army "at the very centre of the Empire" (107). He comes "from the edge of the world" but, as he is careful to remind us, there is nothing marginal or inferior about his origins "of royal blood." However, even though "he had been summoned to serve this state; to lead the Venetian army" (107), his valour and nobility are mostly invisible to his supposedly sophisticated hosts and he finds himself on the margins of Venetian society, spending most of his time in isolation. The unexpected status as an outcast perturbs him: "I found it difficult to reconcile myself to this new emotion of loneliness, and, for the first time in my life, I found myself battling bouts of despondency that could persist for weeks" (117). At the heart of his solitude lies the awareness of being regarded as a mere foreigner whose role is simply to assist a surprisingly parochial, self-involved

Venetian aristocracy to maintain its position of power within the local social hierarchy:

> My former language teacher had explained to me how Venice was controlled by a small hereditary aristocracy. [...] My own position in Venice could be explained by the fact that the republic preferred to employ the services of great foreign commanders in order that they might prevent the development of Venetian-born military dictatorships. In fact, it was common practice to humiliate and break outstanding Venetian soldiers so they did not rise above their station. (116)

Though he provides information about himself, this narrator never states his name. Nonetheless, readers may easily recognize a strong resemblance with the "noble Moor in the service of the Venetian State," the main character in Shakespeare's tragedy. Still, Phillips offers the following clue to identifying the character (cf. 2.1.2.3; 2.2):

> OTHELLO: A play by William Shakespeare. Probably written between 1602 and 1604, and first performed in 1604. The principal source for the play is Giraldi Cinthio's *Hecatommithi*, a collection of Italian stories first published in Venice in 1566, and used by a number of Elizabethan and Jacobean dramatists as source material for their plots. Out of one key sentence in Cinthio's story, Shakespeare wrote the early scenes of the play.
>> It happened that a Virtuous Lady of wondrous beauty called Disdemona, impelled not by female appetite but by the Moor's Good qualities, fell in love with him, and he, vanquished by the Lady's beauty and noble mind, likewise was enamoured of her. (166)

In light of the correspondences observable in the two literary texts, it may be worth taking a moment to briefly list the resemblances as well as dissimilarities between them. An obvious parallel lies in both characters' skin colour. Shakespeare introduces his character as "the Moor," while the novel suggests the character's colour through the statement that he comes "from the edge of the world [...] From the dark margins" (107). Some seventy pages later, the character refers to his West African roots when he recalls a "Yoruba [...] saying" (181). In the first lines of the section devoted to him, the dark-skinned General affirms his noble status as well as his past "as a poor slave" (107). Likewise, in Shakespeare's tragedy, Othello informs the Duke and the "fair lady" Desdemona of his experience of being bought and sold as property: "Of being taken by the insolent foe; / And sold to slavery, and my redemption thence, / And with it all my travel's history" (*Othello* 1.3).

The quasi-Othello too marries the "fair Desdemona" (165) – "the senator's daughter" (125) – who at their first meeting "sat silently, but with a welcoming smile about both her mouth and, more importantly, her eyes. A stranger soon learns that where the mouth may deceive, the eyes tell nothing but the truth." In both texts, public perceptions of a person's character carry greater weight than actual facts. For instance, Iago – "Othello's Ancient" – misleads everyone into believing in his honest intentions and is unquestionably trusted by Othello. Driven by grudge, Iago takes advantage of his reputation and succeeds in making the General unfoundedly jealous.

In Phillips's novel, the quasi-Othello's "outstanding reputation as a General" (127) allows him to be "paid handsomely to be a soldier and a leader of men" (132) despite his skin colour. His dark complexion, however, becomes an obstacle in his attempts to integrate into Venetian society:

I had made no friends among these people, and my standing in society rested solely upon my reputation in the field. My reputation. It was to be hoped that this one small word might lay to rest any hostility that my natural appearance might provoke. My reputation. (118)

In Shakespeare's tragedy, Othello, blinded by jealousy, kills Desdemona. Phillips, by contrast, depicts a strong-minded individual. Eventually, the quasi-Othello realizes that, despite his marriage and his efforts to be accepted in a European society, he will always remain a foreigner in Venice. He is aware that his enduring status as a foreigner places him in a vulnerable situation, an easy target of suspicion and hostility. This growing realization of his powerlessness and isolation gives rise to thoughts of self-preservation and escape to his "own people" (118). His yearning to belong, and, simultaneously, to preserve his identity are accompanied by a sense of existential threat because according to the "Yoruba [...] saying: the river that does not know its own source will dry up" (181).

The quasi-Othello's impulse to leave a place that exhibits xenophobia and deprives him of his identity echoes, to some extent, the young Phillips's intention to leave Britain:

I already sensed that in order to progress I would have to remain particularly vigilant about the way in which my identity was being buffeted and twisted by societal forces. Like any black child in Britain who grew up in the sixties and seventies, it had long been clear to me that the full complexity of who I am – my plural self, if you like – was never going to be nourished in a country which seemed to revel in its ability to reduce identity to clichés. [...] one's identity is traduced and a great violence is done to one's sense of self. [...] I had to get out of this country which seemed determined to offer me only unpalatable, and racially determined, stereotypes as models for my own identity. ("Necessary Journeys" 123-25)

Like the quasi-Othello in the case of Venice, Phillips understands that Britain does not show any intention to integrate the "Other." In the multicultural British society of the eighties, the "Other" is a depersonalized entity, a mostly shapeless non-white component of the larger whole.

Unlike the author, who moved with his West Indies parents to the "mother country" at the age of four months, the quasi-Othello resembles what we currently define as a skilled worker migrant who voluntarily moves to another country with the prospect of improving his life and career primarily for economic reasons. According to the quasi-Othello's résumé he "had led the fighting men of [his] own people for many years, and had also served in battle as a General for several other nations, both Christian and heathen" (121). His military honours and impressive accomplishments earn him an invitation to an important post that would traditionally have entailed a fancy welcoming ceremony. The reality, however, is unpretentious:

> But now I was confidently arriving in Venice, summoned by the doge and his senators to lead the Venetian army whenever the Turks declared their intent. But where was the party to meet me? The fanfare? The escort of lavishly attired gondoliers that were widely known to welcome dignitaries? It appeared that I would have to make do with the spectacle of the city herself turning out to greet me. (121-22)

The lack of courtesy expressed towards the African General is part of a pattern of general indifference to the foreign-born character by Venetians. Their apparent lack of interest masks their barely concealed disdain and occasional "petulant displays of bad manners" (135) towards their black-skinned guest which is in contrast with his desire to be integrated in Venetian society: "My daily routine developed and involved much exploration on water and foot, and then private study, as I grew to master this new language" (114-15). This sense of rejection begins to take a physical toll on the foreign General: "It was this desire to be accepted that was knotting my stomach and depriving me of sleep" (122). He also makes the effort to conform to local customs and fashion. When, for example, he eventually receives the invitation to attend dinner at the Doge's Palace, he is careful to observe Venetian dress codes:

> I therefore decided to spend a good portion of what money I had accrued on acquiring a new costume in order that I might dress myself according to the Venetian fashion, as opposed to that of my native country. [...] I wondered if my new costume might convince some among these Venetians to look upon me with a kinder eye. [...] I am a big man, and I had already noted that a response of some sort upon my joining a room was invariable. In fact, I had come to expect this of my unarmed entrance into any circle. However, [...] the senator moved towards me with his arm outstretched. He announced my name, although I was sure that those present had already been informed of my impending arrival. Clearly, I was to be the chief amusement of this evening. (119-25)

As soon as the quasi-Othello joins the other guests his hopes of gaining approval crumble one more time and give way to the feeling of being the outsider in the limelight. The attempt to dress according to the local fashion is an expedient defined by Jacques Lacan as mimicry:

> Mimicry reveals something in so far as it is distinct from what might be called an itself that is behind. The effect

of mimicry is camouflage, in the strictly technical sense. It is not a question of harmonizing with the background, but against a mottled background, of becoming mottled – exactly like the technique of camouflage practised in human warfare. ("Line" 99)

The African General is on a personal mission to adopt the ways of his hosts, so, perhaps not surprisingly for a military officer, he camouflages his appearance, not with the intent to conceal his personal outfit from the enemy, but in order to make him blend in with his Venetian surroundings. He does not perceive the host country as the enemy. The attempt to camouflage has more to do with his need for overcoming the "new emotion of loneliness" (117), as well as his high regard for the host country, which he views as superior to his native land. It is a perception that started to take hold as soon as Venice became visible to his eyes from the sea:

I arrived in the spring and was immediately enchanted by this city-state. I approached by water and found myself propelled by the swift tides across the lonely empty spaces of the forbidding lagoon. [...] I discovered myself being sucked into the heart of Venice. What ingenuity! Nothing in my native country had prepared me for the splendour of the canals [...] The magnificence of the buildings that lined the canals overwhelmed my senses, and upon the grandest of these buildings, proud images of the Venetian lion were carved in wood, chiselled in stone, or wrought in iron. I could barely tear my eyes from the genius of these palaces, for they suggested to me the true extent of my journey into this fabled city. (106-07)

The quasi-Othello feels simultaneously captivated by and inferior before the magnificence, beauty and power exhibited by the city-state (106). His initial admiration for "the Most Serene Republic of Venice" (48) and his sense of achievement at having made it to "the very centre of the empire" (107) gradually give way to feelings of exclusion and inferiority, which is conveyed by the often repeated sentence "I was clearly not one of their own" (129).

As was the case with other European Empires, the Republic of Venice manages the diversity of its immense territories by the imposition of hierarchies and group disparities starting with the distinction between the ruler and the ruled. In this manner, diversity is governed according to a theory of rank. The European presumption of its own superiority exercizes its authority through, in Young's words, "exploitation of backward or weak peoples" (*Empire* 53) and strict class divisions. Although the General's accomplishments and background should have exempted him from being relegated to a "backward or weak" category in the host country and, unlike his father-in-law, he "was born of royal blood, and possessed a lineage of such quality that not even slavery could stain its purity" (158), as a foreigner his status is reduced to that of unsophisticated, albeit very highly skilled, guest worker.

The quasi-Othello allows Phillips to portray a less obvious, less familiar form of subjugation. The case is not about uprooting the so-called backward or weak peoples to exploit for forced labour. The quasi-Othello voluntarily puts his talents into service of a foreign armed force. As an individual he is clearly in no way inferior to any other Venetian; on the contrary, when judged according to the criteria of Venetian upper-class membership, he can unquestionably consider himself equal to, even superior to, most Venetians. And yet, the Venetian aristocracy snubs him on the grounds of his origins. He is deliberately ostracized and depersonalized into an instrument of war. By the end of the evening at the Doge's palace he clearly perceives his role as prized asset in another's bid for recognition and status:

my invitation to dine at his home had provided those close to him with an opportunity to judge his prize acquisition. He was, of course, sure that he had not made a mistake in hitching his fortune to mine, but to insure himself against future difficulties he was simply seeking approval from his family. Perhaps this was the Venetian custom. (127)

In the span of time between his arrival and the Turks' declaration of war, the quasi-Othello progressively becomes aware of his paradoxical double image as a cosmopolitan, powerful leader and a primitive guest from the ends of the earth. This disquieting epiphany bewilders him. Nonetheless, he attempts to bridge the gap between the two cultures, African and Venetian, that simultaneously manifest themselves in the same range of time and space. In doing so, it may be argued that the quasi-Othello symbolizes what Bhabha defines as "the in-between space" or a space where two different mentalities and ways of life collide ("Vernacular Cosmopolitan" 139). In point of fact, his struggles to negotiate between the antithetical feelings of belonging-longing, inclusion-exclusion are not different than those experienced by descendants of colonized people who moved to, or were born in the "mother country" or any other Western society.

The emotional distress resulting from trying to navigate an in-between space where the experience and ways of the home country pull the newcomer's movement one direction while the norms and expectations of the host country send her or him on an entirely different course is a central concern of postcolonial literature.

At this stage, it may be worth briefly referring to a few novels which treat similar themes as *The Nature of Blood*. Their focus is the movement from different corners of the British Empire to Britain itself and the alienation these migrants feel lost in a country that had proudly identified itself as a global economic power and example of civilization to its colonial subjects. In order to overcome the feeling of being unwanted and excluded, these migrants try to reproduce their original environment in the host country because this gives them back their sense of belonging. They attempt to reproduce home through small daily gestures that replicate those of their country of origin, or by holding on to objects brought from home, objects which might include, for instance, the suitcase they carried with them when they left their home country. The luggage is left visible in their bedroom like a piece of furniture and as a token of an imminent return home.

In Andrea Levy's *Small Island*, for instance, the Jamaican character Hortense arrives in the mother country with a trunk "of the size of the Isle of Wight" (13) jammed with objects and clothes from her village. However, in sharp contrast to the hopes and optimistic dreams that that content may represent, disappointment accompanies Hortense from the instant her "feet had set down on the soil of England" (15). Already on the first morning, in the attempt to cope with the unexpected reality, she finds comfort in one object that powerfully recalls the atmosphere of her birthplace:

> I opened my trunk. The bright Caribbean colours of the blanket the old woman had given me in Ochi leaped from the case. The yellow with the red, the blue with the green commenced dancing in this dreary room. I took the far-from home blanket and spread it on the bed. (226)

The suitcase is associated with home and the feeling of belonging in *The Nature of Blood* as well. In the Cypriot context, when Eva realizes that she soon has to leave the detention camp she rejects the suitcase offered and the implied pretence that still possesses remnants of her old pre-camp life and home:

> It is evening. I am supposed to be packing a suitcase for a journey in the morning. But this is not my suitcase. To

> whom does this suitcase belong? It does not matter, for I have nothing to put in the suitcase. I will be holding my few possessions, much like Mama. *A suitcase suggests a life.* It seems appropriate that I should emerge into the world clutching a bundle. I kick the suitcase. I am not bitter. I just do not want to pretend. Not now. Not ever. Mama will be expecting me in the big city by the river. In the market square. But she will have to see me without a suitcase. (41; emphasis mine)

The rude awakening many migrants experience in Britain is well depicted in the BBC television adaptation of Levy's *Small Island*. The historical drama opens in London, in 1948, at the West India Docks. Hortense sits on a bench with her trunk nearby while waiting for her husband, Gilbert. A voice-over alludes to the expectations shared by the newcomers from the former colonies: "Put the word 'mother' in front of the word 'country' and you think of somewhere safe where your potential will be nurtured and your faults excused" (*Small Island*, dir. John Alexander). In actual fact, what the two Jamaican protagonists discover is a dishearteningly different reality, something which is summarized later on by Gilbert: "I realize that this mother country about which we Jamaicans know so much does not even know where her own children live. She does not care one jot for us."

We find a retreat into familiar gestures of home as a response to the blatant ignorance and lack of concern manifested by the mother country in the movie *Anita and Me* (2002; dir. Metin Hüseyin) based on the semi-autobiographical novel (1997) of the same title by Meera Syal. The novel looks at the relationship between a Punjabi girl with her English neighbour Anita. The movie version is particularly successful in visually rendering the immigrants' attempt to replicate their daily routine and traditions and to maintain their beliefs and values. This self-protective avoidance of the unsympathetic dominant culture on the part of first generation migrants places Meena, the British-born daughter of Punjabi immigrants, in a grey, in-between space where she is forced to navigate constantly between two types of identities.

In literature, testimonies of rituals that establish a temporary sense of belonging by replicating old habits and longed-for spaces from one's past are frequent. In Samuel Selvon's *The Lonely Londoners*, for instance, the jovial male characters find respite from the sense of alienation they experience in the mother country through camaraderie with fellow West-Indians and unchanging weekly routines that predate their arrival in England. For example, the omniscient narrator informs the reader that "every Saturday morning [...] all the spade housewives go to buy [...] They getting on just as if they in the market-place back home" (65). The narrating voice's reproduction of the creolized form of English with its unconventional grammar and richness in slang expressions (spade, for instance, is one of the terms used by Jamaicans to refer to themselves) adds to its Afro-Caribbean migrants' authenticity. Another version of coping with the antithetical feeling of belonging/longing is shown by the character of Tolroy, who carries his guitar everywhere as a way of remaining connected to the calypso music from his birth place: "when Tolroy did left Jamaica he bring a guitar with him to Brit'n, and he always have this guitar with him playing it in the road and in the tube, and when he standing up in the queues" (6). Tolroy plays his guitar in typically in-between situations like "queues" or daily commutes, moments of transition, when he probably feels isolated in the presence of other British citizens. This image of the West-Indian immigrant playing his music in public is yet another instance of re-creating a safe, hospitable, congenial place, a simulacrum of home.

Elsewhere, it is a culinary cultural habit that is depicted: "'Is a long time I ain't eat pigeon, boy,' Galahad say. 'Pigeon meat really sweet,' Moses say. In about a hour they was eating pigeon and rice" (120). This episode denotes not only desperation but also a spontaneous, carefree attitude at the same time. Being hungry and penniless has led Galahad to propose to Moses, a fellow Trinidadian, to reproduce an event that reminds them of their island.

Even in the case of those who have chosen uprootedness, the need of belonging is never very far away. An example is given in the post 9/11 novel, *Home Boy* (2010) by H.M. Naqvi. The narrator, Chuck, is one of three young Pakistani men who live in New York City. When Chuck is about to give up the American dream, he is offered a job just days before his work visa expires. Notwithstanding this guarantee of employment, he has to go back to Karachi and wait for a letter from the American company that will allow him to return legally to the U.S.A. When he returns to New York, at the airport he picks a taxi based on the driver's look. The choice falls on a fellow Pakistani who "knows what you are about [...] he tells you about the *dhaba* in Jackson Heights that serves the best plate of *nihari* this side of the Atlantic. You find comfort in his familiarity with the American Way of Life" (215). The phrase "knows what you are about" indicates Chuck's need to feel understood and connected to his origins in a foreign country, even though he is in New York entirely by choice. Upon his arrival in the largest, most cosmopolitan city in the United States, Chuck thinks of Karachi where "there you were yourself and you were alive. Now you feel lonely, you despair" (216). The taxi driver empathizes with his passenger and, in a paternal way, recommends the roadside restaurant where Chuck can eat Pakistani stew and where the owner's cultural background will make him feel secure like any human being feels within a group of individuals who share common roots. Chuck's craving for a taste of Pakistani food and companionship in New York provides him with connection to something recognizable and real from his previous life before immersing himself in his new American life.

Literature, as suggested by Phillips's works, to some extent mirrors this figurative stepping forward (into a new culture)-stepping back (into one's roots) movement. Literature, like a sympathetic fellow countryman or food, can also convey the tangible, material connection between individual and place of origin. Niyi Osundare does so in *The Eye of the Earth* (1986). In his poetry, Africa is given an anthropomorphic shape, she is Mother Nature and the nurturer of her people: "I [...] suckled on the delicate aroma of healing herbs. [...] Earth was ours, and we the earth's" (*Eye* 22).[3] The earth envisioned in Osundare's writing is fertile and generous, it is as if the umbilical cord that provides nourishments is never cut. In addition, Osundare's verses describe another type of mother, this mother can be patient and unconditionally welcome her children:

> The rocks rose to meet me
> like passionate lovers on a long-awaited tryst.
> [...]
> "You have been long, very long, and far",
> [...]
> The rocks rose to meet me
> Tall rocks, short rocks
> sharp rocks, round rocks:
> [...]
> The rocks rose to meet me
> Eloquent in their deafening silence ("The Rocks Rose to Meet Me" 52-58)
> [...]
> distant trees wave orange hands
> to a homing prince ("Eyeful Glances" 72)

The image of the rock suggests stability and firm foundation while the trees are personified as an adoring crowd welcoming their wandering child. Furthermore, despite the rocks' oxymoronic "deafening si-

---

[3] This collection of nineteen poems is devoted to mother earth and other forms of physical nature. It mainly focuses on the relationship between human beings and their environment. It sheds light upon Mother Nature as the source and nurturer of egalitarian relationships in contrast to human beings' habit of exploiting their natural resources for their own profit.

lence," the alliteration of the sound "r" bestows a sort of rhythmic, musical reception on their "homing prince." This is in sharp contrast to what happens in the mother country, which is detached and indifferent to her children's feelings. What is more, that mother country, as Osundare points out, "crashed in from across the seas, with a blind sword and a crown of noisy gold, smashing old customs, assailing the very core of ancient humanistic ethos" (preface 22). Osundare's poetry can be interpreted as an expression of a longing for dignity both for Africans and for their place of birth, that is to say their point of origin, the same point of origin evoked by the bond between a biological mother and her offspring. In doing so, an anthropomorphic connection between people and place is established, a bond that embodies the timeless human yearning for a sense of belonging. The association of Africa with Mother Nature implies a relationship with one's land of birth that is rooted in and is perceived as an extension of the natural environment of the continent. This understanding of one's life and origins as being tied to a larger natural world is in a way reflected in the quasi-Othello's comparing himself to a river that the Most Serene Republic of Venice will eventually dessicate.

Before realizing the extent to which his "foreign adventure" (182) is a threat to his roots, the quasi-Othello devotes considerable effort and time trying to conform to Venetian culture. From observing the world, he learns that

> For the aristocratic Venetian marriage was a carefully controlled economic and political ritual, and it was therefore important to keep the bloodlines pure. This being the case, prostitution was not only tolerated but positively encouraged, for it enabled the aristocratic man to indulge his desires without endangering the sanctity of his class. (112)

Once again, we are presented with a dark-skinned migrant confronted with a highly stratified society in which "the sanctity of [the dominant] class" is preserved through amoral, unwritten rules that allow and conveniently justify another form of exploitation: prostitution. This calculating, unsentimental concern with preserving the *status quo* at any cost exposes a rift between the African soldier's experience in his homeland and what he observes in Venice. In his native culture, protecting class privilege takes a secondary role to emotional bonds with one's spouse and children:

> I [...] cast my mind back to the wife and child that I had left behind in my native country.[4] I did not think of myself as having spurned them, for they were in my heart and would evermore remain there. As was the custom with a warrior, there had been no formal marriage, it being understood that at any moment I might lose my life. (It was never understood that at any moment I might also lose my heart.) My son would forgive me, for in a few years he, too, would be a man and follow in his father's footsteps. (134)

During the dinner given for him at the Doge's palace, the quasi-Othello is introduced to the host's family members. The encounter with one particular family member acts on the emotions of the foreigner attendee to such an extent that on his way to his lodgings he fears he has been the victim of some mysterious sorcery: "I felt as though, against my will, some part of my soul had been captured" (128). The quasi-Othello fantasizes not only about a future life with the governor's beautiful daughter but – in a display of utilitarian stra-

---

[4] This passage allows the reader to draw a parallel with Stephan. Both characters are envisioned as a hub connecting heterogeneous historical events and both sacrifice their personal relationship with their family and surrender to what they perceive as a greater cause: the establishment of a Jewish home for Stephan and a military career in the case of the quasi-Othello.

tegic thinking not unlike that practiced by the local ruling class – he hopes that the marriage may advance his standing and integration into Venetian society:

> In my quieter moments, I had often wondered if a marriage of the finest of my own customs with their Venetian refinement might not, in due course, produce a more sophisticated man. Or, if not this, perhaps such a conjunction of traditions might at least subdue a portion of the ill-feeling to which my natural state seemed to give rise. (120)

One obstacle the quasi-Othello longs to overcome is the prejudice against what he refers to as his "natural state." Some lines further down, he shows signs that he has begun to internalize the racism he is experiencing when he associates his darker complexion with an undesirable defect or debasement that requires erasing: "The stain of my smoky hand on her marble skin, a mark that might be washed clean in the milky basin of family love" (146). At this point in the story, the quasi-Othello is still naively optimistic that feelings of love will have the transformative power he yearns for despite evidence that emotional considerations have little purchase with the Venetian aristocracy.

The Nature of Blood is not the only work in which Phillips offers for consideration the issue of interracial relationship/marriage. In his play *The Shelter* (1984), for instance, he specifically focuses on

> the story of the black man and the white woman [that] in the Western world is bound together with the secure tape of a troubled history; and the relationship between the black man and the white woman has always provoked the greatest conflict, the most fear, the most loathing. (10)

In the quasi-Othello the wish for such a relationship causes the "desire to be suddenly *white*" (Fanon, *Black Skin* 45; emphasis in the original). As Kwame Anthony Appiah (foreword ix) observes, Fanon explores the issue of "identity created for the colonial subject by colonial racism." This imposed mental construct based upon the superiority of the white colonizer over the black colonized leads the subjugated individual to reject "the fact of [their] own blackness" (ix). One way the black man imagines he may overcome his sense of inferiority is if he is loved by the white woman:

> I want to be recognized not as *Black*, but as *White*.
> But [...] who better than the white woman to bring this about? By loving me, she proves to me that I am worthy of a white love. I am loved like a white man.
> I am a white man.
> Her love opens the illustrious path that leads to total fulfilment...
> I espouse white culture, white beauty, white whiteness. Between these white breasts that my wandering hands fondle, white civilization and worthiness become mine.
> (*Black Skin* 45; emphasis in the original)

Fanon's reflections on interracial relationships can be applied to the quasi-Othello's assessment of whether his situation has in fact changed now that the white daughter of a nobleman has reciprocated his love:

> Then I fell to one knee and sealed our union with the tenderest of kisses. Was I truly the same man who had arrived lonely and unannounced? The same man who had sailed in a state of spellbound wonder right into the heart of this city-state? The same man who had enter-

tained a willing but subtle Venetian whore[5] at the suggestion of my first 'master', even though I derived little pleasure from my actions? The same man who had initially struggled with the language, and who had, at times, wondered if he would ever settle among these strange and forbidding people? And now to be married, and to the heart of the society. I wondered how such a change could be wrought in a man's life, and in so short a period. (144)

The quasi-Othello is experiencing a sense of detachment from his own self as he undertakes what he believes is the ultimate step towards attaining whiteness. However, as soon as he, in Fanon's words, "espouse[s] white whiteness" (45) the African General manifests a shift in attitude that is characterized by arrogance and male chauvinism. Pondering his new position within Venetian society, he regards his wife as sort of coveted trophy, a prize wrenched from the grasp of others at a great cost: "I now possess an object of beauty and danger, and I know that, henceforth, all men will look upon me with a combination of respect and scorn. I also know that never again will I be fully trusted by those of my own world, both male and female" (148). Nonetheless, if on the one hand the "object of beauty" suggests a form of ownership; on the other hand, Fanon's reflections allow a further interpretation: the object symbolizes "white civilization and worthiness" (45) which can be achieved by the black man through the white woman's love.

The "white" African General's objectification of his young wife contrasts with his earlier feelings. He thought of streets and material

---

[5] "The woman whom my merchant deemed suitable to play host to my natural instincts was pleasant enough, and conversation formed part of her trade with me" (112). In point of fact, the dark-skinned General spends their time together enquiring about Venetian culture, including more intimate aspects of life in the host state: "upon my urging, [she] began to explain to me the rules of courtship that are peculiar to Venetians of all classes" (112).

landmarks as something more than mere physical objects when he compared the empty city of Venice to a peaceful, vulnerable child:

> It had, after all, long been my custom to explore the strange regions of this enchanted city, often mistaking the way, probing the network of back streets and the complex labyrinths of alleyways in search of both new and familiar landmarks. At night, when abandoned to serenity, her breathing light and regular, Venice presented herself as a sleeping babe upon whom one might spy with proprietorial glee. (120)

The personification of the city in this passage could be read to the effect that contrary to the worldly materialism that pervades Venetian culture, the African General still has not lost his ability to perceive life and human feeling even in the stone buildings and alleyways of a deserted city. But his words can also be interpreted in a less sentimental manner. The adjective 'proprietorial' evokes a fixation on ownership. What is more, the image of Venice as a sleeping child passively displayed to be gazed at for one's pleasure is a fairly familiar male-entitled and male-centred view of female beauty. This alternative understanding is reinforced by the semantic field of words employed by the quasi-Othello to express "her" attractiveness:

> I had grown extremely fond of the city under the moon, for it was at such moments that I truly appreciated the full grandeur of her silent majesty [...] With the sea behind me, I clipped forwards at a good pace, until the city began to show herself [...] the people [...] thoroughly unaware of the privilege of living among such overwhelming beauty [...] the spectacle of the city herself [...] the city herself, which had remained ever faithful to her enchanted promises. (121-22)

In their study on Shakespeare's plays set in Venice – *The Merchant of Venice* and *Othello* – Bassi and Alberto Toso Fei (50-52) indirectly provide an explanation for the quasi-Othello's shift in perceiving and addressing Venice as a woman. According to them, the reason for this anthropomorphizing of the Italian city is traceable to Graeco-Roman mythology and its deity associated with beauty, love, pleasure, passion and procreation. In regard to Shakespeare's plays the goddess in question is Venus who stands for a common denominator to Cyprus and Venice. The former is commonly known as the goddess' birthplace, whereas the latter is conjoined with Venus by reason of assonance due to their Latin etymology: *Venetia, Venetiae* versus *Venus, Veněris*. Furthermore, legend has it that, like Venus, Venice was born of seafoam, even though its birthdate goes back only to March 25, 421, with the sun in Aries and Venus as rising sign. Evidence related to mythology and the war-love dichotomy is present in Shakespeare's tragedy. Desdemona, for example, is simultaneously identified with the god of war by the Moor ("O my fair warrior!"; 2.1) and Iago ("Our general's wife is now the general"; 2.3) and the goddess of love with whom Othello falls in love.

This brief digression into the myth behind Venice and its merging into literature allows a supplementary comparison between the Elizabethan tragedy and *The Nature of Blood*. As illustrated earlier, the interracial relationship at the core of Shakespeare's work is borrowed and rearranged by Phillips. He reshuffles the plot elements and portrays a reverse situation. Venice and Desdemona function as a magnetic field that exerts a great attraction for the newcomer "at the very centre of the empire" (107). Nonetheless, as time goes by, within that magnetic field the gravitational pull slowly inverts its route. As a consequence, this change in direction/sentiment makes the strong-minded African General rebuff the lure of female beauty in favour of an eventual return to his origins. If we carry the parallel between the myth and the novel further, it may be argued that the god of war personified by the quasi-Othello prevails against the goddess of love personified by both Venice and Desdemona.

The African General's "custom to explore the strange regions of this enchanted city" (120) leads him also to the Jewish quarter:

> It occurred to me that this was the district about which my merchant had spoken, the place where the money-lenders resided, and never having entered this quarter, I was keen to satisfy my curiosity while everybody slept. The two Christian guards were naturally suspicious about my approaching them, but seeing that I was clearly not one of their own, and that I did not seem intent upon harming any Jew, they unbolted the gates and, after I had bestowed upon them a small token of my gratitude, they let me pass. (129)

The African General and the Jewish community represent two forms of the "Other" in Venice. Although relegated to the edges of Venetian society, they are in fact indispensable actors in the life of the Republic without whom it would be difficult to preserve political prestige and economic power. As Ledent (142) points out, unlike the attentive reader, the African General "is unable to view the Jewish ghetto as a warning of the way Venice, and Europe, deal with strangers like him."

As far as the African is concerned, he is only able only to register a prejudice against his skin colour. In the above passage, his colour indicates to the Christian guards that he is not a member of the Jewish community. In addition, being the "Other" and consequently regarded as inferior, the African is regarded as too insignificant to either be contaminated by contact with non-Christians or to threaten the *status quo* in any way, which explains why the guards do not stop him. Thus, they grant both the character and the reader admission to a restricted area and to a moment in the narrative where two historical realities converge: the African and Jewish diasporas, embodied by the quasi-Othello and the residents of the ghetto respectively.

The quasi-Othello's observations of the Jewish reality within the ghetto reveals a community without the rigid class demarcations that define Christian Venetian society. The apparent lack of social distinctions is more a function of the over-crowded living conditions imposed on the Jewish citizenry than an explicit intention on the part of the residents of the ghetto to erase class divisions. The Christian authorities' refusal to recognize the inherent human richness and complexity of the Jewish community's social organization is a deliberate tactic employed to categorize Jews as less refined, unsophisticated and clearly separate from Venetians.

In Nazi Germany the state-promoted, intentional denial of all individual and class difference in the minority Jewish population had reached a new level of elaboration and genocidal violence. In *The Nature of Blood*, Eva is witness, like the quasi-Othello in the Jewish quarter centuries earlier, to the eradication of any form of distinguishing traits among Jewish detainees (161; cf. 2.1.2.2). In the Venetian ghetto, the African outcast not only remarks on the urban and architectural aspects of the Jewish quarter, but also informs readers of the restrictions imposed on Jews, who are compelled to live "locked behind gates" (129). Unaware of the parallels between his own status as the "Other" and the situation of the ostracized Jews – parallels that become obvious to the reader now that the two realities have intersected in this stroll through the Jewish quarter –, the African continues his exploration and mentions a recurrent edict that emerges from those prohibitions, namely, the ban from any form of interaction with the host community: "Intimacy between Jewish men and Christian women was punishable by a heavy fine and up to twelve months' imprisonment, depending upon whether the woman was a public prostitute" (129). During his wandering through the ghetto, the General describes the prison-like neighbourhood in the military terms that reflect his professional background as well as in the bigoted language of his

Christian hosts: "the Jews were herded *en masse* and enclosed in one defenceless pen" (129). The semantic field of animals and animal husbandry employed here has over the centuries invariably been associated with the so-called inferior peoples, such as Jews, and evidence of such a superior-inferior relationship is vividly conveyed in Eva and Malka's accounts of events, and are also alluded to in the quasi-Othello's story (cf. 2.1.3; 3.1).

As soon as the African General introduces himself, he declares his previous status as that of "a poor slave" (107). This piece of information is not just mentioned upon his arrival in Venice. On the contrary, he mentions it every time he wishes to emphasize that he is chiefly a human being who "was [also] born of royal blood, and possessed a lineage of such quality that not even slavery could stain its purity" (158). The quasi-Othello does not suffer from the obsessive adherence to the inflexible social categories that dominate the Venetian world view. For him there is no paradox in being both a noble and a former slave, an African and a future Venetian. Conversely, for his European hosts, class lines are fixed and immutable. As an outsider in Venice he is forever confined to the role of "them." To most sixteenth-century Europeans, a slave is a material commodity and virtually impossible to conceive as a normal Venetian, much less a nobleman.

In his study of current forms of slavery, Pietro Deandrea (4) calls attention to the "1982 UN updated definitions of slavery: [...] slavery is any form of dealing with human beings leading to the forced exploitation of their labour." This reminds us that slavery remains a commonplace reality for many people to this day. Official definitions do not always reflect evolving and existing circumstances. Nevertheless, the essence of slavery remains analogous. The slave was generally someone outside the dominant group, someone categorized as lower in status and often of a different ethnicity, nationality and religion from his owner. The condition of social differentiation and/or stratification was, and still is, essential for slavery to flourish. As a general rule, there has to be a perceived labour shortage. However, especially in the past, the abundance of free lands and open resources waiting to be commodified often represented a prerequisite for slavery. The historical data that confirms slavery's persistence in human history is mentioned by the quasi-Othello during the dinner at the Doge's Palace:

> Venetian households did, from time to time, use black slaves. I countered with the information that I had once been held as a slave, yet, as unpleasant as this situation had been, I had survived to tell the tale. I watched this boy carefully and, deciding that the victory was already secured, I chose not to mention my royal blood, or the fact that many Romans and Greeks had also been held as slaves. (126)

Nowadays, the number of people worldwide who are subjected to some form of slavery is estimated in the millions. Although Deandrea's study (177-202) focuses primarily on the present-day British context, slavery remains well rooted in human nature and his research is applicable to all Western countries whose *élite* classes operate on a globalized scale and continue to benefit from labour exploitation of vulnerable workers in developing countries as well as in Western civilized societies. At the current time, slavery (or unfree labour) continues through practices such as debt bondage – the most widespread form of slavery today – and domestic servants. Their status as illegal workers renders them invisible and victims of abuse, humiliation, not to mention frequent dehumanizing comparisons between undocumented foreign labourers and animals. Vulnerable people who leave their home country for various reasons are subject to forms of physical and psychological violence replicating in this manner the enduring relationship between master and servant (Deandrea 33-47).

This digression allows me to shed light on the African General's previous status as a slave. Given that slavery is a global phenomenon, it is not surprising to find instances of slave owning communities in Africa as well. The African slave culture is evidenced by the number of texts that deal with the issue of servitude such as that by Olaudah Equiano and *Paradise* (1994) by Abdulrazak Gurnah, to name just two. Equiano's memoir informs readers of the details of his voyage on a slave ship, the brutality of slavery in the colonies of the British Empire, his settling in London and how he became a leading abolitionist in the seventeen-eighties. Consistent with the conventions of the literary genre Equiano has chosen, his memoir is based on Equiano's personal experiences and observations starting from his Nigerian childhood. He tells readers about his abduction and the numerous times he changed masters. Gurnah's *Paradise* follows the story of a Tanzanian boy named Yusuf at the turn of the twentieth century. The young Yusuf is pawned in exchange for his father's owed debt to Aziz and must work as an unpaid servant for the merchant:

> Khalil told him, 'You're here because your Ba owes the seyyid money. I'm here because my Ba owes him money' [...] 'How much did your father owe him?' Yusuf asked. 'It's not honourable to ask,' Khalil said [...] 'And don't say *him*, say seyyid.' [...] 'He ain't your uncle,' Khalil said sharply [...] 'It's important for you. He doesn't like little beggars like you calling him Uncle, Uncle, Uncle. He likes you to kiss his hand and call him seyyid. And in case you don't know what it means, it means master.' (24-25; emphasis in the original)

The above conversation is between two indentured workers. The naïve teenager, Yusuf, matures during his bondage to his exploitive Uncle. He learns the ways of the world as he encounters African communities at war, trading safaris gone awry, and the reality of European colonialism. Through Yusuf, readers become aware of a hierarchy both in the colonizer society and in local social groups. Later in the novel, in a gesture that reflects years of socialization as a submissive, acquiescent servant, he voluntarily joins the ranks of the invading colonial German army which is sweeping across Tanzania forcibly conscripting men into its ranks:

> as he watched the obliviously degraded hunger of the dogs, he thought he knew what it would grow into. The marching column was still visible when he heard a noise like the bolting of doors behind him in the garden. He glanced round quickly and then ran after the column with smarting eyes. (247)

It may be argued that Yusuf's story emphasizes the deep-rooted attitude to subjugate and exploit the individual who somehow is regarded as inferior and unworthy of a dignified, human consideration. At this point, it may be worth briefly introducing also the institution of pawnship or the use of people as collateral for credit. The practice of seizing and holding persons, until the debt was duly payed down, was common in West Africa but during the Middle Passage, this practice underpinned the Atlantic Slave Trade. In the seventeenth and eighteenth century, people were used as pawns, which means that they were enslaved, manly for debts or crimes to British merchants/slave traffickers (Lovejoy and Richardson 67-70).

The same Europe that has for centuries produced individuals like Eva or the quasi-Othello – and even Phillips himself – with their "multifarious sense of self [...] burdened with a complicated historical and geographical weight" ("Necessary Journeys" 124-30) is unable or unwilling to establish what Phillips regards as healthy societies:

> Healthy societies are ones which allow such pluralities to exist and do not feel threatened by these hybrid conjoinings. [...] in continental Europe many countries suffer from the same myopia as Britain [...] As a young writer,

travel enabled me to understand that constantly reinterpreting and, if necessary, reinventing oneself is an admirable legacy of living in our modern, culturally and ethnically kinetic world. The most dangerous thing that we can do to ourselves is to carelessly accept a label that is offered to us by a not always generous society that seeks to reduce us to little more than one single component of our rich and complex selves. ("Necessary Journeys" 131)

The Nature of Blood is an act of resistance against this urge that seeks to reduce people and history to simplistic labels and self-serving narratives of cultural/racial superiority. The novel offers a pluralistic, multi-faceted investigation of past events; but it is also, simultaneously, an exploration of human nature and an attempt to understand the mechanisms that lead certain individuals and communities to fear, reject as equal and ruthlessly exploit their fellow humans.

Appendix
A Conversation with Caryl Phillips

The following conversation took place in Caen, May 23, 2017 on the occasion of a conference on Caryl Phillips, "Inhabiting the Voids of History," at which I presented a paper on *"The Nature of Blood* and fragmented history."[1]

My original intention was to interview Caryl Phillips focusing on *The Nature of Blood*. I arrived at the appointment with my list of questions, but as soon as I was in front of him, in front of a warm, very accessible, relaxed human being sipping his cup of coffee, I completely forgot about my carefully laid out plan and found myself involved in a conversation. We were simply two people talking mainly about his novel, and because of this, for me, unexpected but very agreeable turn of events, digressions seemed to be unavoidable. On a previous occasion, Caryl Phillips had told me "I'm *all* about digressions." This interview is further confirmation of this. Unfortunately, the limited time available to our conversation did not allow me to pursue all questions on my mind.

MF: My first question is on intertextuality, because for someone like you who has been and still is an avid reader most of the time intertextuality is unconscious and unintentional, but in your novels, most of the time you make clear references to authors and their works and I was wondering if this is a form of praising or a form of acknowledgment like the ones you find at the beginning or at the end of a book when the writer thanks all the people who supported him/her during his/her working process; or, is it a sort of "writing back to the author,"

---

[1] The conference was organised by professor Françoise Kral in the framework of the *Agrégation d'anglais* 2017-2018. The official programme 2017-2018 included Caryl Phillips's *Crossing the River* (1993).

an emulation of "writing back to the Empire" as practiced by postcolonial writers like Achebe, for instance?

CP: I think it is probably more an attempt to engage with, and somehow destabilize, the English canon. If you can engage with it, but also make people try and see it in a new way, thus destabilizing it, you are inevitably taking away some of its authority. The key authors in English Literature have a tremendous hold on the imagination of British people and I am attempting to adjust the strength of that grip by suggesting that their canonical work is, in a sense, a part of my work. In this sense it is conscious, but I don't think it is something that authors have done frequently in English, but they have done so in other languages, the French for example. Of course, in recent times, Coetzee has done it in English. It's a way of making the reader see things afresh, which is after all what literature is, a way of making you see the world anew. In this instance, part of what the reader is looking at anew is the so-called canon.

MF: May I define *The Nature of Blood* as one of your most challenging novels so far?

CP: You mean formally?

MF: Yes, I mean formally

CP: Probably. When I delivered that manuscript to my publishers in America, I think they were kind of horrified because the two books that had come before, *Cambridge* and *Crossing the River*, had sold, you know for me, a lot of copies. To look at it from a strictly commercial point of view, which I don't, I had an audience. I had people waiting for the next book, and I think I surprised my so-called audience with this book, because a lot of people found it challenging and I couldn't (or wouldn't) make the connections that the form and structure demands. I feel sure publishers wanted another book that was formally, and in terms of subject-matter, in the tradition of *Cambridge* or *Crossing the River*. But, you know, I've never really worried about how many books I've sold. I actually don't know how many copies a book sells and I don't care. I'm not interested if I sell ten or if I sell ten thousand. Obviously I would prefer to sell ten thousand, but I don't really care because the hard thing – the important thing – is to write the book, and when I write a book I just hope that somebody will want to publish it and thereafter somebody might read it. If I had been writing *The Nature of Blood* before *Cambridge* and before *Crossing the River* I think I might have had some problems getting it published.

MF: In *The Nature of Blood,* I was wondering ... to me the intended target seems to be the British Empire for its steady presence in history along with its steady presence in other forms of colonialism and oppression. Is this kind of perception correct, or not?

CP: I don't know if I would say that it is an intended target as such, I mean because ...

MF: receiver, maybe, or someone you were addressing the novel ...

CP: Well in some way, I think that everything I ever write is addressing British imperial notions of colonial history – a history that excludes me – so I think I am always trying to be a little bold and say "look at me, look at me over here, you know my story matters too, my experience matters too." I think that there is some aspect of that in everything I write, but I never begin a story actually *thinking* that way. I always begin and pursue a story thinking of the characters, I never think of the themes. Themes are what other people tell you about when they are trying to work out what's going on in the novel. I just think well I have got this character called Eva and I have got this other character called whatever he or she is called, and I've got to make them reveal the story and grow. Literally that's all I ever try to do, I let the characters lead. However, inevitably, if you publish a number of books, people are not stupid, and they can see thematic links from one book to another book. In this sense themes are present, I can't say they don't exist, but I can definitively say I am never thinking of them too consciously while I am writing a book.

MF: This leads me to my next question about characters, because in your novels the words employed to present and describe a character make them a real human being and not a fictional one, you reveal the character with common imperfections and weaknesses and this in turn allows your reader to better identify with the characters, at least this is what I get from your books, how does a character take shape in your mind?

CP: Slowly, really slowly. I don't even know I have a character fully realized until I hear the character's voice. The key element is the voice; when I know exactly how a character speaks, what words they use, for instance would they ever swear? Furthermore, what words would they *never* use because they might consider those words to be too vulgar. When I can answer these questions then I am beginning to really understand a character. I need to *feel* the rhythm when they're speaking. I need to know if they have an accent. Once I can hear the voice then I know that I have a character, but I also have to know a lot that's never in the book. If you were to ask me a series of questions such as what car do they drive? In fact, do they drive a car? And if they do drive a car, what colour is the car? What make is the car? I would have to be able to tell you the answers to these questions. I have to know the characters well enough to know irrelevant things, such as where would they go to shop for clothes? Would they ever consider buying clothes from a second-hand shop? Would they consider spending three hundred euros on a pair of shoes? What would they say to somebody who would spend three hundred euros on a pair of shoes, or would they even talk to such a person? I need to know the answers to these *irrelevant* questions even if the specifics never find their way into the book. However, the one thing that's *absolutely* necessary is hearing the voice.

MF: Stephan Stern in *The Nature of Blood*, he is an activist, he joins Zionism for the cause of the "promised land." Have you inserted him in the narration as a probable counterpart of Pan-Africanism? If yes, among diasporas, specifically African and Jewish diaspora which are the most known, debated and discussed, what is today your position on the issue of Pan-Africanism? Has anything changed from the year you wrote and described it in *The Atlantic Sound*?

CP: My feelings on Pan-Africanism haven't changed. In many ways they are similar to how I feel about Christianity or religion in general. It is very hard to be too critical of something that enables people to survive the many problems of life. If people believe in a system that enables them to wake up in the morning and function as normal human beings, and such a belief system enables them to be kind to others and enables them to have a positive vision of the world, who am I to object? Pan-Africanism is not something I personally believe in. I like the idea of unity, I like the idea of people having more in common with each other, but some ideas feel a little idealistic to me. Pan-Europeanism hasn't worked, as we've just been reminded with Brexit, and Africa is much, much bigger than Europe. How are all the African diasporan people of the world, be they from the Caribbean, or Brazil, and so on, supposed to seriously think they are going to have any meaningful interaction with each other around the idea of a mythical and often ahistorical notion of Africa? In truth, it's a nice idea but when you examine it closely there are many, many problems. And that's how I feel about religion too. It's a nice idea and it enables people to live, and so on. I'm not criticizing it, but when you examine it really closely there are some glaring illogicalities. Coming back to Pan-Africanism, we have to accept that race – being of the African continent – constitutes just one element of our identity and so to base much of one's life-decision-making process around this element is somewhat reductive. To do so misses out so many other things ... so that's about how I feel about it to be honest.

MF: ... and, sorry going back once again to the novel, did you see Israel as a probable counterpart of Africa?

CP: Yes, I was aware of the multiple ironies of placing Africa next to Israel. In other words, what it means to try and build a society and a sense of self around one construct of identity which, as I've said, seems to me to be too narrow a way of looking at oneself and society. People are more complicated than just what religion or what ethnicity they are. It's complicated. One may argue that what Pan-Africanism movement maybe tried to do, the Israelis have pulled it off. But is it successful? Well, it enables some people to get through the day, but I have been to Israel a couple of times and didn't feel comfortable and I left the country early. I simply didn't like the idea of a state where identity was principally built around just one thing. I saw young Israeli children carrying machine guns who were militarized and I thought, "no, don't do that to the children, don't do that to them. This is not healthy."

MF: In regard to African history ... sometimes reading between the lines, I had the feeling you were saying that, maybe, Africa is the only continent that does not have history, have I perceived it correctly?

CP: Africa has a history, but it is not a history that people properly recognize. Africa certainly has a long and complex history, it is just that it's largely ignored by the West.

MF: And are you still struggling with this Western inability of understanding it?

CP: Well, no. A lot of the reasons for not understanding this history are simply rooted in prejudice and ignorance. There are many, many fine African writers struggling to address this ignorance.

MF: Ehm, Africans don't have a proper recognition yet, but, I don't know, sometimes it seems to me that contemporary African people seem to be passive, as they have accepted the idea of being subjugated, still nowadays ...

CP: No, I don't think so.

MF: But things in Africa went, have gone and still are going from bad to worse ...

CP: But that's not necessarily the fault of the African people. They have been dealt a very bad hand historically. You can argue, yes there's corruption etc. but it would be very harsh to look at African history and come to the conclusion that, well, they are *not* trying. The news gets worse, the poverty level increases, the life expectancy doesn't appear to be going up at the right pace, but many of these issues have to be understood through the lens of the past. It's like African-American society in the US, which is still enduring great problems; the fact is, you don't recover from two or three hundred years of slavery in three or four generations. It takes a *long* time to recover from that kind of systematic subjugation. That is how it is with Africa, centuries of colonial subjugation and exploitation are undeniable and you can't really recover from this in a few decades. So, it doesn't surprise me that large parts of Africa are still bedevilled by corruption, poverty, malnutrition, and diseases of various kinds, but it's only been fifty or sixty years of independence for many countries; balance that against three hundred years of somebody basically screwing with you, exploiting all your minerals, drawing lines on maps, setting tribes against tribes, bringing over diseases that people had never known before and that they are not able to fight off and deal with. Just because you've got a new flag now and a national anthem it doesn't mean that you can immediately make an in-road into three or four hundred years of colonial subjugation. Fifty years is really a brief span of time when you set it against the historical legacies that African people are dealing with. So, I just think ... it will take time for Africa, but I think Africa will be ok; it will just take time, certainly more time than we have in our lifetimes. You're not going to necessarily see massive great change in a lifetime, and if you do you are very lucky. For instance, people in South Africa did. If you were living in South Africa in the last twenty-five years, yes, you witnessed something incredible, but the positive consequences of that change are going to take hundreds of years to take hold. It's not going to happen immediately. All radical and positive redressing of such historically-determined socio-economic and political imbalance requires both action *and* patience.

MF: To you writing is a means of establishing a sort of one-way communication channel with your readers? Or a tool that is able to confer a voice to your thoughts, reflections and feelings with the intent to budge awareness in readers? Because, sometimes people tend to be lazy. Reading your novels is challenging. Is this an effort, a commitment that you require from your readers?

CP: I just think that we've become very lazy as a society in the last twenty years or so because of social media and because of the Internet. We don't even spell properly anymore because of texting, and we don't have the same attention. That said, I can only be true to a certain form of literature which may be perceived by some people as being challenging and difficult, but if people feel this way they don't have to read the books. If they don't want to spend the energy or make the effort then so be it. Hopefully, if they do read the work and expend the energy they will get something out of it. When I was a student I remember reading challenging work and thinking, "damn, this is hard going. I'm not having lot of fun with this," but eventually I got something out of it. Does it mean that it was pleasurable? Not always. But if you're looking for an easy ride, then you wouldn't buy *The Nature of Blood* or *The Lost Child*. To my mind the reader has to make an investment; the reader has to pay attention and contribute. If the reader doesn't want to do this and they simply want to be entertained then they should read something else. After all, there's nothing wrong with doing that.

MF: Sorry, something more on your act of writing, writing is a way to confer a voice to your thoughts and reflections? Is it something you want to share with your readers? Or it is something in your DNA...

CP: Well, I'm not sure it's in my DNA. I think I only write because I have something to say and I've always thought to myself that when I don't have anything to say I won't write because there are already too many people out there writing books. I took up writing because I *felt* strongly that I had something to say, but I know the price of saying that something. It has involved spending long periods of time by myself writing, so sometimes I just think I would like a different type of life, a more well-balanced – that would be the phrase – type of life.

MF: Ehm, back to your characters, you said before introducing the character to the reader you have at first to learn as many details as possible about him/her, and it seems to me that you, maybe, intentionally leave the reader the possibility to formulate his/her own judgement, opinion on the fictional character. For instance, in *The Lost Child*, the character of Monica's father, he is so human, he has more flaws than virtues, he is strict, square-minded, but at a certain point you seem to raise the possibility he could have been a paedophile.

CP: It seems to me that Monica is going through more than just the normal adolescent "I need to break from my parents" kind of rebellion that most of us go through. Furthermore, there seems to be something slightly sexually repressed about her father. You didn't get the idea that he is having a particularly jolly sex life with his wife, so I began to think about this guy. He looks to me like the type of man who might have a hidden agenda. He's just one of those guys that on the surface seem very conventional, but if you scratch a little bit you might find something else. Now we don't know if Monica's suspicions are real, but that's the thing about fiction, we can make up our own mind. Personally, I think it's quite possible that he made some kind of unpleasant overture to one of Monica's friends. He's the kind of man that might have done that, but it's not clear that he did. As you know, you can't prove most of these allegations, a teacher making a pass at the student is hard to prove it because there's only two people, nobody else is in the room, and it becomes his word against her word. It's often the same with similarly serious allegations such as rape, there are no witnesses, so you have to look and make a decision about the characters. Who do you think who is believable here, what's likely, what's possible? Well I think it's a similar situation that we have with Monica's father. Monica has an oblique, vague feeling, but whether it's plausible or not, whether it's believable or not just depends on your reading of Monica's father. One might read him as an absolute creep, or else just think "oh, come on, the guy is a bit square, where's the evidence that he is some kind of sexual predator?" So you can read it whichever way you want depending on, of course, who you are or what life experience you bring to the novel.

MF: And this kind of leaving things hanging is intentional, isn't it?

CP: Yes, I can't solve it, because that's how it is in life. I mean if Monica was saying, "he murdered somebody," these kinds of allegations are usually resolved one way or another. You know, you're guilty or not guilty. It's like a traffic ticket for speeding, you're guilty or not guilty. Evidence is produced and it's often difficult to argue against it. One of the reasons why issues of sexual harassment are so difficult is there are usually no witnesses. With Monica's father we just don't know, no evidence is presented, but my sense is Monica has a strong feeling, and anything beyond this depends on how you perceive of both Monica and her father.

MF: ... he is also someone who has difficulties in engaging socially.

CP: Yes, which may well be why he would do something like that – pick on a young person who has little power – and proceed on the basis that they won't say anything because they're frightened to report him. If he is a man who has difficulty engaging socially he might do that rather than doing the normal thing which is to say to your wife, "I don't know if this marriage is working, we need to ..." or conversely saying to his secretary "Do you want to go to the motel tonight?" Making a pass at a young girl who has no power in his eyes, might be his way forward. You know, men can be creepy like that.

MF: Out of curiosity, scholars always perform a sort of autopsy on your works, why are you not interested in their analysis?

CP: Because it doesn't help me to write. It's not because I don't think their analysis is valid or insightful or worthwhile, I'm grateful that people read the work and want to write about it critically, but scholarly work doesn't help me to write another novel and if it doesn't help me write another book then I don't have to read it. I know that some writers read feedback looking for praise and in the hope that people say nice things about them, but when people don't say nice things those writers have got to read that too, otherwise it is not fair to just read the good things. Were I to choose to read the bad reviews *and* the positive feedback, then I would just be riding a kind of roller-coaster. To my mind it's pointless and actually distracting. Obviously, without criticism literature would be a lot less rich. After all, writers need feedback, you need people to take the work seriously, but you've got to be sensible and give scholars the room to work freely. The last thing a scholar or a critic needs is somebody telling them, "no, you got it wrong." Actually, they didn't get it wrong, it's their interpretation and so did they get it wrong? I have a chance when I'm writing a book to have it all my own way and to arrange things how I want, but when I've handed over the book to somebody, whatever emotions or critical response it provokes is beyond my control and it's not for me to worry about this. I know it's a strange analogy I'm going to make, but when Beethoven finished the Fifth Symphony it's thereafter none of his business whether people listen to it and cry every evening, or whether they listen to it and throw up because they hate it. It's not about Beethoven anymore, it is about the work. Now if he needs to know how people feel about his work in order to know how to write the Sixth Symphony then fine! Personally, I don't feel involved in a book once I've finished it, therefore why am I going to try and disturb scholars, or myself, by worrying about their interpretation of something that is finished and behind me? If critics want to check with me, like you're doing, and other people have done in the past, fine, I will often have a chat about the work. But I would never say, "No, you're absolutely wrong." I might say "no, you thought that this idea emerged out of that, but no, I wasn't thinking of that," but I don't think I would be dismissive or overly defensive.

Works Cited

Agamben, Giorgio. *Homo Sacer: Sovereign Power and Bare Life*. 1995. Trans. Daniel Heller-Roazen. Stanford: Stanford UP, 1998.

Andrews, Kehinde. "Beyond Pan-Africanism: Garveyism, Malcom X and the End of the Colonial Nation State." *Third World Quarterly* 38.11 (2017): 2501-2516, DOI: 10.1080/01436597.2017.1374170. Published on line 20 Sep. 2017.

Anita and Me. Dir. Metin Hüseyin. Icon Film Distribution, 2002.

Appiah, Kwame Anthony. Foreword. *Black Skin, White Masks*. By Frantz Fanon. vii-x.

Arendt, Hannah. *The Origins of Totalitarianism*. 1951. Orlando, Austin, New York, San Diego, London: Harcourt, 1973.

———. "We Refugees." 1943. *Altogether Elsewhere: Writers on Exile*. Ed. Marc Robinson. Boston London: Faber and Faber, 1994. 110-19. < https://www.arendtcenter.it/en/2016/10/11/hannah-arendt-we-refugees-1943/>. Accessed 1 Nov. 2017.

Banton, Michael and Jonathan Harwood. *The Race Concept*. London: David & Charles, 1975.

Barthes, Roland. *Camera Lucida: Reflections on Photography*. 1980. Trans. Richard Howard. London: Vintage, 1993.

———. *Il grado zero della scrittura, seguito da Nuovi saggi critici*. 1953. Trans. Giuseppe Bartolucci, Renzo Guidieri, Leonella Prato Caruso, Rosetta Loy Provera. Turin: Einaudi, 2003.

Bassi, Shaul. *Essere qualcun altro: Ebrei postmoderni e postcoloniali.* Venice: Cafoscarina, 2011.

———."Oltre la 'razza.'" *Gli studi postcoloniali: Un'introduzione.* Ed. Bassi and Sirotti. 101-24.

———, and Alberto Toso Fei. *Shakespeare in Venice: Luoghi, personaggi e incanti di una città che va in scena.* Treviso: Elzeviro, 2007.

———, and Andrea Sirotti, eds. *Gli studi postcoloniali: Un'introduzione.* Florence: Le Lettere, 2010.

———, and Isabella di Lenardo. *The Ghetto Inside Out.* Trans. John Francis Phillimore. Venice: Corte del Fontego, 2013.

Bauman, Zygmunt. *Modernity and the Holocaust.* Cambridge: Polity, 1989.

"Belsen Concentration Camp 1945." *The National Archives Website.* <https://www.nationalarchives.gov.uk/education/resources/belsen-concentration-camp/#external-links>. Accessed 15 Nov. 2017.

"Bergen-Belsen." *Holocaust Encyclopedia.* United States Holocaust Memorial Museum, Washington, DC. <https://encyclopedia.ushmm.org/content/en/article/bergen-belsen>. Accessed 15 Nov. 2017.

Bhabha, Homi K. *The Location of Culture.* 1994. London and New York: Routledge, 2004.

———. "The Vernacular Cosmopolitan." *Voices of the Crossing: The Impact of Britain on Writers from Asia, the Caribbean and Africa.* Ed. Ferdinand Dennis and Naseem Khan. London: Serpent's Tail, 2000. 133-42.

Bibby, Harold Cyril. *Race, Prejudice and Education*. London: Melbourne, Toronto: Heinemann, 1959.

"Biography." *Caryl Phillips: Official Web Site*. <https://www.carylphillips.com>. Accessed 15 Nov. 2016.

Browning, Christopher Robert, with contributions by Jürgen Matthäus. *The Origins of the Final Solution: The Evolution of Nazi Jewish Policy, September 1939-March 1942*. Lincoln: U of Nebraska P, Jerusalem: Yad Vashem, 2004.

Canetti, Elias. *Crowds and Power*. 1960. Trans. Carol Stewart. New York: Continuum, 1978.

Caruso, Paolo. *Conversazioni con Lévi-Strauss, Foucault, Lacan*. Milan: Mursia, 1969.

———. "Conversazione con Michel Foucault". 1967. *Conversazioni con Lévi-Strauss, Foucault, Lacan*. By Caruso. 91-131.

Clingman, Stephen. "Forms of History and Identity in *The Nature of Blood*." *Salmagundi* 143 (2004): 141-66. DOI: 10.2307/40549575. Published on line Summer 2004.

Cole, Teju. *Blind Spot*. 2016. Trans. Gioa Guerzoni, *Punto d'Ombra*. Rome: Contrasto, 2017.

Dawson, Ashley. "To remember too much is indeed a form of madness: Caryl Phillips's *The Nature of Blood* and the Modalities of European Racism". *Postcolonial Studies* 7.1 (2004): 83-101. DOI: 10.1080/1368879042000210612. Published online 7 Aug. 2006.

Deandrea, Pietro. *New Slaveries in Contemporary British Literature and Visual Arts: The Ghost and the Camp*. Manchester: Manchester UP, 2015.

Dennis, Ferdinand, and Naseem Khan. *Voices of the Crossing: The Impact of Britain on Writers from Asia, the Caribbean and Africa.* London: Serpent's Tale, 2000.

Eddo-Lodge, Reni. *Why I'm No Longer Talking to White People About Race.* 2017. London: Bloomsbury, 2018.

Equiano, Olaudah. *The Interesting Narrative of the Life of Olaudah Equiano, or Gustavus Vassa, the African.* 1789. Ed. Vincent Carretta. London: Penguin, 2003.

Fanon, Frantz. 1952. *Black Skin, White Masks.* Trans. Richard Philcox. New York: Grove, 2008.

_____. *The Wretched of the Earth.* 1961. Trans. Constance Farrington. New York: Grove, 1963.

Fergusson, Niall. *Impero: Come la Gran Bretagna ha fatto il mondo moderno.* 2003. Trans. Anna Luisa Zazo. Milan: Mondadori, 2009.

Frank, Anne. *The Diary of Anne Frank. 1942-1944.* Ed. Michael Marland and Christopher Martin. Harlow: Longman, 1989.

Freud, Sigmund. *An Autobiographical Study, Inhibitions, Symptoms and Anxiety, The Question of Lay Analysis and Other Works.* Trans. James Strachey. The Standard Edition of the Complete Psychological Works of Sigmund Freud. Vol. 20 (1925-1926). London: Hogarth, 1959. <https://www.freudpage.info/autobiographical_ study.html>. Accessed 8 Nov. 2017.

_____. *Moses and Monotheism.* Trans. Katherine Jones. Hertfordshire: Hogarth Press and the Institute of Psycho-Analysis, 1939.

Ghert-Zand, Renee. "At Bergen-Belsen, where tens of thousands perished... and others began their lives," *Times of Israel*, 27

April 2015. <https://www.timesofisrael.com/in-the-cemetery-at-bergen-belsen-a-walk-among-anonymous-ghosts/>. Accessed 15 Nov. 2017.

Gilman, Sander L., and Steven Theodore Katz. *Anti-Semitism in Times of Crisis.* New York: New York UP, 1991.

Gilroy, Paul. "Suffering and Infrahumanity." *The Tanner Lectures on Human Values.* <https://tannerlectures.utah.edu>. Accessed 10 Oct. 2018.

Gurnah, Abdulrazak. *Paradise.* 1994. London, New Delhi, New York, Sydney: Bloomsbury, 2004.

Hall, Stuart. *Cultura, razza, potere.* Ed. Miguel Mellino. Verona: Ombre Corte, 2015.

———. "Razza, articolazione e società strutturate a dominante." Translation of "Race, Articulation and Societies Structured in Dominance in Sociological Theories: Race and Colonialism." 1980. Trans. Eleonora Meo. *Cultura, razza, potere.* By Stuart Hall. 67-124.

Hannaford, Ivan. *Race: The History of an Idea in the West.* Baltimore: Johns Hopkins UP, 1996.

"Harriet Tubman". *Encyclopædia Britannica Online.* <https://www.britannica.com/biography/Harriet-Tubman>. Accessed 25 June 2018.

Hart, Alan. 2009. *Sionismo il vero nemico degli ebrei.* Vol. 1. *Il falso Messia.* Trans. Diego Siragusa. Milan: Zambon, 2015.

Herman, Judith Lewis. *Trauma and Recovery.* New York: Basic, 1992.

Hesse, Isabelle. "Colonizing Jewishness? Minority, Exile, and Belonging in Anita Desai's *Baumgartner's Bombay* and Caryl Phillips's *The Nature of Blood*." *Textual Practice* 28.5 (2014): 881-99. DOI: 10.1080/0950236X.2013.858072. Published on line 13 Dec. 2013.

Howe, Stephen. *Afrocentrism: Mythical Pasts and Imagined Homes.* London, New York: Verso, 1998.

Hughes, Derek. "Blackness in Gobineau and Behn: *Oroonoko* and Racial Pseudo-Science." *Women's Writing* 19.2 (2012): 204-21. DOI: 10.1080/09699082.2011.646867. Published online 13 Feb. 2012.

Joyce, James. *Ulysses.* 1922. Ed. Jeri Johnson. Oxford: Oxford UP, 1993.

Kalowski, Marcello. *Il Silenzio di Abram: Mio padre dopo Auschwitz.* Rome-Bari: Laterza, 2015.

Kapuściński, Ryszard. *L'altro.* 2006. Trans. Vera Verdiani. Milan: Feltrinelli, 2015.

Kinni, Fongot Kini-Yen. *Pan-Africanism: Political Philosophy and Socio-Economic Anthropology for African Liberation and Governance.* Vol. 3. Bamenda: Langaa, 2015.

Knutsen, Elise. "Israel Forcibly Injected African Immigrants with Birth Control, Report Claims." *Forbes* 28 Jan. 2013. <www.forbes. com>. Accessed 20 Apr. 2017.

Lacan, Jacques. "The line and the light." 1973. *The Four Fundamental Concepts of Psychoanalysis.* By Lacan. Trans. Alan Sheridan. London: Chatto & Windus, 1977. 91-104.

Ledent, Bénédicte. *Caryl Phillips.* Manchester: Manchester UP, 2002.

Levy, Andrea. *Small Island*. London: Headline Review, 2004.

Long, Edward. *History of Jamaica*. 1774.

Lovejoy, Paul, and David E. Richardson. "The Business of Slaving: Pawnship in Western Africa, c. 1600-1810." *Journal of African History* 42.1 (2001): 67-89.

Mbembe, Joseph-Achille. "Necropolitics." *Public Culture* 15.1 (2003): 11-40.

_____, and Sarah Balakrishnan. "Pan-African Legacies, Afropolitan Futures: A conversation with Achille Mbembe." *Transition* 120 (2016): 28-37.

Mellino, Miguel. Introduction. *Cultura, razza, potere*. By Stuart Hall. 7-22.

Miller, James. *The Passion of Michel Foucault*. New York: Anchor, 1994.

Morrison, Toni. *The Origin of Others*. Cambridge, Massachusetts: Harvard UP, 2017.

Naqvi, H.M. *Home Boy*. New Delhi: Harper Collins India, 2010.

Osman, Khan Touseef. "Trauma and Fiction: Representational Crises and Modalities." *Crossing: A Journal of English Studies*. 8.1. (2017): 160-67.

Osundare, Niyi. *The Eye of the Earth*. 1986. Trans. Pietro Deandrea. *L'occhio della terra*. Italian and English edition. Florence: Le Lettere, 2006.

_____. Preface. *L'occhio della terra*. By Osundare. 22-28.

_____. "The Rocks Rose to Meet Me." *L'occhio della terra*. By Osundare. 52-60.

_____. "Eyeful Glances." *L'occhio della terra*. By Osundare. 69-74.

Paci, Enzo. *Diario Fenomenologico*. 1961. Milan: Bompiani, 1973.

Phillips, Caryl. "Afterword to the Vintage Edition". *The European Tribe*. By Phillips. 130-34.

_____. *The Atlantic Sound*. 2000. London: Vintage, 2001.

_____. "Anne Frank's Amsterdam." *The European Tribe*. By Phillips. 66-71.

_____. "Blood." *Color Me English: Migration and Belonging Before and After 9/11*. By Phillips. 167-72.

_____. *Cambridge*. 1991. London: Vintage, 2008.

_____. *Color Me English: Migration and Belonging Before and After 9/11*. New York, London: New Press, 2011.

_____. "Color Me English." *Color Me English: Migration and Belonging Before and After 9/11*. By Phillips. 3-17.

_____. "Conclusion: The 'High Anxiety' of Belonging." By Phillips. 303-09.

_____. *The European Tribe*. 1987. New York: Vintage, 2000.

_____. "The European Tribe." *The European Tribe*. By Phillips. 119-29.

_____. "Fire." *Color Me English: Migration and Belonging Before and After 9/11*. By Phillips. 173-82.

_____. "In the Ghetto." *The European Tribe*. By Phillips. 52-55.

_____. "How much more of this will we take?" *The European Tribe*. By Phillips. 92-99.

_____. Introduction. *Heart of Darkness & Selections from the Congo Diary 1857-1924*. By Joseph Conrad. Introd. by Caryl Phillips. New York: Modern Library, 1999.

_____. "A Life in Ten Chapters." *Color Me English: Migration and Belonging Before and After 9/11*. By Phillips. 107-12.

_____. *The Lost Child*. London: Oneworld Publications, 2015.

_____. *The Nature of Blood*. New York, Toronto: Alfred A. Knopf, 1997.

_____. "Necessary Journeys." *Color Me English: Migration and Belonging Before and After 9/11*. By Phillips. 123-31.

_____. *A New World Order*. London: Secker & Warburg, 2001.

_____. Preface. *The European Tribe*. By Phillips. ix.

_____. *The Shelter*. London: Amber Lane, 1984.

_____. *A View of the Empire at Sunset*. London: Vintage, 2018.

Purchase, Sean. *Key Concepts in Victorian Literature*. Basingstoke: Palgrave Macmillan, 2006.

Qresel, Elyāqîm-Geşel. *Zionism*. 1973. Bloomington: Indiana UP, 2008.

Riesigl, Martin, and Ruth Vodak. *Discourse and Discrimination: Rhetoric of Racism and Antisemitism*. London: Routledge, 2001.

Robinson, Marc. *Altogether Elsewhere: Writers on Exile*. Boston, London: Faber and Faber, 1994.

Rosenberg, Beth. "The Postcolonial Jew." *Synthesis* 8 (Fall 2015): 32-46.

Rothberg, Michael. *Multidirectional Memory: Remembering the Holocaust in the Age of Decolonization.* Stanford: Stanford UP, 2009.

Richman, Sophia. "Finding One's Voice". *Contemporary Psychoanalysis* 42.4 (2006): 639-50. DOI: 10.1080/00107530.2006.10747136. Published on line 31 Oct. 2013.

Rylance, Rick. *Roland Barthes.* Hemel Hempstead: Harvester Wheatsheaf, 1994.

Sartre, Jean-Paul. Preface. *The Wretched of the Earth.* By Frantz Fanon. 7-31.

Scego, Igiaba. *Adua.* Florence: Giunti, 2015.

Scego, Igiaba. *Adua.* 2015. Tans. Jamie Richards. New York: New Vessel, 2017.

Schacter, Daniel L. *Searching for Memory: The Brain, the Mind, and the Past.* New York: Basic Books, 1996.

Selvon, Samuel. *The Lonely Londoners.* 1956. London: Penguin, 2006.

Shakespeare, William. *The Merchant of Venice.* Ed. John Russell Brown. London: Cengage Learning, 2007.

Shakespeare, William. *Othello, The Moor of Venice. The Complete Works of William Shakespeare.* 1996. Shakespeare Head Press, Oxford, Edition, 1999. 818-57.

Shindler, Colin. *Triumph of Military Zionism: Nationalism and the Origins of the Israeli Right.* London, New York: I.B. Tauris, 2009.

Siragusa, Diego. Prefazione. *Sionismo: Il vero nemico degli ebrei.* Vol. 1. *Il falso Messia.* By Alan Hart. 5-18.

Small Island. Dir. John Alexander. BBC One, 2009.

Syal, Meera. *Anita and Me.* Glasgow: Harper, 1997.

wa Thiong'o, Ngũgĩ. *Decolonising the Mind: The Politics of Language in African Literature.* 1986. Oxford: James Currey; Nairobi: EAEP; Portsmouth (NH): Heinemann, 2005.

_____. *In the House of the Interpreter: A Memoir.* 2012. London: Vintage, 2013.

Young, Robert J. C. *Empire, Colony, Postcolony.* Chichester: Wiley & Sons, 2015.

_____. *Postcolonialism: A Very Short Introduction.* Oxford: Oxford UP, 2003.

STUDIES IN ENGLISH LITERATURES

Edited by Koray Melikoğlu

ISSN 1614-4651

1 *Özden Sözalan*
 The Staged Encounter
 Contemporary Feminism and Women's Drama
 2nd, revised edition
 ISBN 3-89821-367-6

2 *Paul Fox (ed.)*
 Decadences
 Morality and Aesthetics in British Literature
 2nd, revised and expanded edition
 ISBN 3-89821-573-3

3 *Daniel M. Shea*
 James Joyce and the Mythology of Modernism
 ISBN 3-89821-574-1

4 *Paul Fox and Koray Melikoğlu (eds.)*
 Formal Investigations
 Aesthetic Style in Late-Victorian and Edwardian Detective Fiction
 2nd, revised and expanded edition
 ISBN 978-3-89821-593-0

5 *David Ellis*
 Writing Home
 Black Writing in Britain Since the War
 ISBN 978-3-89821-591-6

6 *Wei H. Kao*
 The Formation of an Irish Literary Canon in the Mid-Twentieth Century
 ISBN 978-3-89821-545-9

7 *Bianca Del Villano*
 Ghostly Alterities
 Spectrality and Contemporary Literatures in English
 2nd, revised editon
 ISBN 978-3-89821-714-9

8 *Melanie Ann Hanson*
 Decapitation and Disgorgement
 The Female Body's Text in Early Modern English Drama and Poetry
 ISBN 978-3-89821-605-5

9 *Shafquat Towheed (ed.)*
 New Readings in the Literature of British India, c.1780-1947
 ISBN 978-3-89821-673-9

10 Paola Baseotto
"Disdeining life, desiring leaue to die"
Spenser and the Psychology of Despair
ISBN 978-3-89821-567-1

11 Annie Gagiano
Dealing with Evils
Essays on Writing from Africa
2nd, revised and expanded edition
ISBN 978-3-89821-867-2

12 Thomas F. Halloran
James Joyce: Developing Irish Identity
A Study of the Development of Postcolonial Irish Identity in the Novels of James Joyce
ISBN 978-3-89821-571-8

13 Pablo Armellino
Ob-scene Spaces in Australian Narrative
An Account of the Socio-topographic Construction of Space in Australian Literature
ISBN 978-3-89821-873-3

14 Lance Weldy
Seeking a Felicitous Space on the Frontier
The Progression of the Modern American Woman in O. E. Rölvaag, Laura Ingalls Wilder, and Willa Cather
ISBN 978-3-89821-535-0

15 Rana Tekcan
Too Far For Comfort
A Study on Biographical Distance
2nd, revised and expanded edition
ISBN 978-3-89821-995-2

16 Paola Brusasco
Writing Within/Without/About Sri Lanka
Discourses of Cartography, History and Translation in Selected Works by Michael Ondaatje and Carl Muller
ISBN 978-3-8382-0075-0

17 Zeynep Z. Atayurt
Excess and Embodiment in Contemporary Women's Writing
ISBN 978-3-89821-978-5

18 Gianluca Delfino
Time, History, and Philosophy in the Works of Wilson Harris
2nd, revised and expanded edition
ISBN 978-3-8382-0265-5

19 Taner Can
Magical Realism in Postcolonial British Fiction: History, Nation, and Narration
ISBN 978-3-8382-0724-7

20 Maria Festa
History and Race in Caryl Phillips's *The Nature of Blood*
ISBN 978-3-8382-1433-7

ibidem.eu